Half-Past Winter

Other books by Nancy Hopkins Reily

Sunstone Press:

>*Classic Outdoor Color Portraits: A Guide for Photographers*
>*Georgia O'Keeffe, A Private Friendship, Part I, Walking the Sun Prairie Land*
>*Georgia O'Keeffe, A Private Friendship, Part II, Walking the Abiquiu and Ghost Ranch Land*
>*Joseph Imhof, Artist of the Pueblos*
>*My Wisdom That No One Wants*

Best of East Texas Publishers:

>*I Am At An Age*

Half-Past Winter

Second Beginnings: My Story, So Far

Nancy Hopkins Reily

SUNSTONE
PRESS

SANTA FE

Sunstone books may be purchased for educational, business, or sales promotional use.
For information please write: Special Markets Department, Sunstone Press,
P.O. Box 2321, Santa Fe, New Mexico 87504-2321.

Book and Cover design › Vicki Ahl
Body typeface › Constantia ‹ › Display typeface › ITC Mona Lisa
Printed on acid-free paper
∞

Library of Congress Cataloging-in-Publication Data

Reily, Nancy Hopkins, 1934-
  Half-past winter : second beginnings, my story, so far / by Nancy Hopkins Reily.
    pages cm
    ISBN 978-0-86534-278-1 (softcover : alk. paper)
  1. Reily, Nancy Hopkins, 1934- 2. Photographers--Texas--Biography. I. Title.
TR140.R415A3 2013
770.92--dc23
[B]
                              2013007167

WWW.SUNSTONEPRESS.COM
SUNSTONE PRESS / POST OFFICE BOX 2321 / SANTA FE, NM 87504-2321 /USA
(505) 988-4418 / ORDERS ONLY (800) 243-5644 / FAX (505) 988-1025

Dedicated

To my family members when they become senior citizens. I hope they greet their "senior moments" with laughter, whether their senior moments are a lapse in memory or a term meaning "the time in your life" to enjoy the fruits of your labor.

Contents

Preface

Nancy Hopkins Reily thought she knew everything she needed to know when she published *I Am At An Age* in 1990 at age fifty. She says, "I had compiled my life's experiences with metaphors using the mountains as background. I approached my experiences as universal experiences that everyone recognized as his life. Six months after the book was published I realized I had more to learn: in-laws, sandwich generation, writing, over thirty-four years of journaling with selective excerpts, sixty-four lines of genealogy, laurels, my aging and grandchildren. I knew I would have to write a sequel."

And here it is, all these years later. She has eliminated most of the metaphors. Some themes continued although homes, clothes and make-up have changed. But her persona has remained the same.

Everyone has a story, It is still her story, so far.

1

The Seasons

My "second beginning" in my life, unplanned, tells me I have much more to learn. I have lived through spring, summer, Indian summer, autumn and now half-past winter.

Spring, growing out of winter, marks the transition from the extremes of winter and to summer. It's easily recognized and I have lived through many killing frosts of winter as the snows thaw and emerge from the mountainsides to create the rivers' highest levels. The angle of the sun's rays, the distance of the sun from the earth, and the length of daylight emerges from the shortness of winter. It is time for new birth and sowing. With the coming of warmth, the flower seeds are nurtured and push through the earth after their long sleep and break through with blossom after blossom. The fresh green on the trees provides a canopy of continuous, ever returning shade as nature's air conditioning.

Summer is quite recognizable as transitional spring ends. The movement of the earth around the sun brings the sun's rays to an extreme angle and a further distance from sun to earth, bringing longer daylight hours. The solstice invigorates the growth of the spring flowers and trees to maturity. I seek the shade in the extreme season.

I enjoy the Indian summer days before autumn as a time for harvesting everything that was sowed in spring and summer. Its days are a little melancholy and sunny, yet autumn's distinctive character allows preparation for the coming extreme pendulum swing. Then the first frost signals the end of summer shadows on the mountains.

Winter, as a time of dormancy, comes as a time for rest although every mile I walk in winter seems like two miles. But too much reflection means that little will be accomplished. I hesitate to enter winter and never want to leave. In contrast to summer, the winter movement of the earth around the sun brings the sun's rays to a lesser angle and shorter daylight hours. This shortened period of sunshine provides a solstice to dormant the earth and provides a circle of quiet.

All these pieces of my life are shaped, condensed and set. Yet, my "flame for life" is alive. I thought I would feel old at half-past winter, but I have a second beginning.

2

A Second Beginning

I return to the mountains which remain the same, to discover all the ways I have changed and find that I have much more to learn. I sit in the flower-strewn meadow by the beaver ponds near my parents' mountain cabin at Elk Creek Ranch in South Fork, Colorado, not doing anything, not moving, only being myself. I have learned to sit quietly because I have the capacity to put my life together any way I chose. Great things can happen when humans and mountains meet.

The pond, like an enormous mirror wedged smoothly among the trees and cradled in the mountains, reflects the naturalness of nature's trees, clouds, mountains and even me. I have seen the reflection of myself, the mountains, the earlier purple aster in the pond as a witness to not only my strength, but now the sudden ripples of water represent the inevitability of movement and change. This reflection forms me and is of everyone I know: family, friends, and acquaintances. It includes every place I have been: to the creek, to the river, to the beaver ponds, to the out-of-the-way road; everywhere I have walked, talked and slept; even the roads I looked down but did not travel. My life and its reflections manage its own weight and I have remnants of every age that I have been. The reflection centers not on materialism but on satisfaction in what I do. My needs, important to me, are possibilities evolving into accomplishments.

When I sat by the pond earlier in my life, I thought I knew all I needed to know about grasping the meaning of life. Yet, there was a precise line dividing one reflection from another. Today I see in the pond the reflections of solid rocks and trees and then a gentle wind ripples the pond and the illusion disappears. The disappointment insists I turn away from the pond to see the real trees and rocks. The earth is my stability. The mountains have taught me much and I have more to learn. My learning skills are not idle, but slower.

Shortly after picking up the purple aster that floats toward me, I begin to move by straightening my body to stand. I am properly dressed for the return walk to my parents' cabin.

I no longer yearn for variety. Today I am overloaded with choices and choosing becomes a distraction. I have no one to blame if I choose badly.

I prepare myself for my travels by choices. The night before my skin is cleaned with a cleansing cream that almost melts to the touch as it penetrates the fine crevices of my face and gently dissolves any foreign particles. The next morning moisturizer and a foundation make-up color that never fades are added because a natural look is part of my persona. My pinkish-red lipstick is applied to my fun loving mouth and doubles for rouge as the pink-red color spreads across both cheeks to form cheekbones any fashion model appreciates. My style is not about getting noticed, but about being remembered. It seems second nature to apply cosmetics to my face for my presence which can be considered the cool, classic side of beautiful.

When I select my Monte Cristo hat, I stand up to get the right proportions, use both hands to try it on, find the balance with my body type and height, and remember that nobody wears a hat better than the British.

My medium-in-size Monte Cristo straw hat with the 13 x 12 inch brim from front to back and twelve inches side-to-side in a medium size fits my head snugly. Earlier I exchanged the multi-colored hat band for navy blue. The blue favors my gray hair better than the sleek, minimalist black. The inside leather band carries my name stamped in gold and misspelled as Nancy Reilly. The tan shoe lace strap when tied under my chin, anchors my hat from the wind. Often my hat sets the tone for my ensemble.

My long sleeve shirt is durable, fits my shape and looks good. The style and color is basic, but I dare not be monochromatic. The full spectrum of colors comes from nature. I dress to enhance my gray hair which demands lots of color to add energy to my presence. A touch of white at the neckline adds the finishing touch.

Depending on my location and itinerary my slacks are somewhat fashionable. Today there is no such thing as a single style of dressing. The rules of dressing now are only guidelines. My slacks are varied from cotton, silk, and nylon. The cotton slacks separate me from the commonplace by the fine cotton twill that is substantial but washes soft to drape close to my body, yet retains a modest shape. My cotton blue jeans often contain elastic to conform to my body's shape. My silk slacks are comfortable to replace the heavy day slacks. Nylon lined with flannel is a favorite when snow blankets the ground.

Today tucked in my cotton slack's side pocket is my white pocket handkerchief and to the untrained eye the hand-stitched and pull-work make it distinctive. My memory of my first handkerchief is when I gathered all the handkerchiefs from my small shallow drawer known as a handkerchief drawer, took out every handkerchief, placed them in an orderly fashion—whites with whites, colors with colors, some not so much embroidered, but embroidery—to view them as a whole. They were a myriad of colors and designs like in a patchwork quilt. More than simple pieces of cloth, they were an extension of my persona.

On any of my outings I want my shoes to fit properly whether they are tennis shoes, walking shoes, or hiking boots. I want a good fit because every time my foot strikes the ground, the force of one-and-a-half times my body weight is under the heel and ball of my foot. If I can move my foot from side to side, the shoe fit is loose; if tight on the sides and instep, it's too snug. I want my shoes to follow the outline of my foot with ample room for my toes to bend and flex. The neutral heel distributes my body weight evenly on my foot bones which are designed to bear the weight resulting in good posture and balance.

Today, on this outing, my shoes are hiking boots. When I bought them, I tested them for the fit by walking up a ramp to check for my heel slipping too much and then walking down a ramp to check if my toes slide forward and hit the front of the boot. The shoes are built for support and flexibility. I wear a much needed ultralight style because my hour trips aren't over rugged terrain.

My wrist watch, a portable mechanical timepiece and dependable companion available by the flip of my wrist, contains a flat steel mainspring that stores energy when the watch is wound. It's more practical than to take out a pocket watch every time. I have the same number of hours a day as Michelangelo and Mother Teresa, but I sense my time is being compressed and as the years go by, time reverses my opinions and I judge not. My watch is visible when I wear my shirt long sleeves rolled up to mid-forearm.

My walk back to my parents' cabin is on the same dirt road

as my arrival, only walking downhill with the wind at my back pushes me onward. My arrival at the cabin fills my memory full of faces, imagined but not present, belonging to my son, daughter, brothers, parents and sisters-in-laws, a daughter-in-law, a son-in-law, and grandchildren—all in four generations. These are not faces collected in a snapshot album but living faces—some steadfast, some happy, some troubled, some reluctant, others believing, and even resilient faces.

Today at my parents' cabin, as never before, too many people arrive and depart in the spring, summer, autumn and half-past winter. If I count the cabin's king size beds as holding two, there are only enough beds for eight.

On this walk back to my parents' cabin, a second beginning tells me it's important to remember how I got here.

3

My Homes

My first home was a white frame cottage on a quiet street in Dallas, Texas. Speaking of Texas, regardless of Texans' bragging, Texans are gracious.

My mother and father, Anna Pauline (Richardson) and Robert Howell (Hal) Hopkins, moved the white frame cottage from behind the Arcadia Theater on Greenville Avenue. The house was cut into sections and hauled to a nearby street, 6030 Vickery Boulevard. This house was our first house with an address ending in an even number. As the house moved down the street, we learned that my father had left his pajamas hanging over the bathtub in the bathroom which was open for all the traffic and neighbors to see. Our future across-the-street neighbor said that the neighborhood marveled at the moving rooms and laughed at Daddy's pajamas on the bathtub.

I was about four years old when Mother and Daddy settled my brothers, Robert who was on the older-brother side of handsome and Morten who was on the younger-brother side of handsome, and me in this well respected suburban neighborhood, but today it is thought of as an inner-city area. The neighborhood at that time was considered an acceptable place to live because the automobile made it easy to get into the city. The area did not have an ethnic mix such as Italian, Jewish or Polish. Only the usual national holidays were recognized, and not holidays such as *Cinco de Mayo* and Martin Luther King Day.

Our street had its rhythms of patterns of trees, houses, and driveways that were familiar as we walked the sidewalk giving us a feeling of control over the neighborhood.

From the front porch, the front door led directly into the living room. At the front of the house next to the living room was a bedroom. Behind the living room was a sun parlor and dining room, followed by the breakfast room and kitchen. Past the kitchen was a back porch with the wringer washing machine. The bathroom for the front bedroom and another bedroom was reached by a hall. Later a third bedroom and bath was added behind the second bedroom.

The house had a wide front porch across the width of the house and acted as a buffer zone between life's challenges and the home's quieter comfort. Four short wrought iron columns supported by larger brick columns supported the porch roof. The steps off the front porch were wide enough for sitting, climbing, and playing games. From the steps, the sidewalk led to the city-provided sidewalk that extended on both sides of the street. The sidewalk was two pedestrians wide allowing people to walk side by side.

The porch was important because it shaded the front part of the house from the sun with its extreme temperatures and allowed us to keep the front windows open for a breeze and for protection from the rain. There was no ceiling fan on the porch and the porch was not screened. On the porch we were neither in the house or out of the house, but in a protected middle ground.

It was a good place for sitting, day dreaming, visiting, people watching, enjoying a cool breeze, keeping a watch on the playing children, watching the cars pass, sipping iced tea, and reading. It also provided a place for us to visit with guests before inviting them inside the house.

The front porch and the sidewalk were part of our social life. It was a pleasant place to entertain our guests. Our guests often were not invited guests, but those who just walked by and said "hello."

We didn't have air conditioning then and neither did anyone else. With no air conditioning, the front porch was the coolest place and where we all congregated.

I remember playing on a hot summer day on the front porch. I would climb on the brick columns, make things and day dream, which one day would became a constant vision I would nurture with passion and determination. The porch often proved useful.

My creative expression surfaced at the age of five years when I received a 9 x 12 inch spiral scrapbook. Of all my childhood things saved, I marveled that this was one of two scrapbooks saved by Mother who was on the engaging side of beautiful, Grandmother Emma Belle Richardson who was on the stately side of beautiful, and me.

Scrapbooking was many things: telling a story, keeping memories, designing and preserving. The hands-on aspect of cutting, gluing, folding, and arranging was a way to create. The scrapbook contained my drawings, greeting cards, pictures I'd cut out of magazines such as babies, food, buildings, cigarette packages, trucks, cars, the 1939 World's Fair, trains, cartoons, and six pictures of fountain pens which may have been an undetected interest in writing.

My second attempt at creative expression was when I was eleven years old and made an 11 x 15 inch scrapbook. It had two Scottie dogs on the red plaid front. Inside I pasted my piano recital programs, my elocution recital program from 1945, my father's Army-Navy E award for excellence in an essential industry in World War II, a football program, my certificate of promotion at Westminster Presbyterian Church Sunday school, National Piano Playing Audition programs, greeting cards, report cards, and a post card from the Taos, New Mexico artist Joseph Imhof.

The scrapbook would carry personal significance for me and my family as it captured milestones in my early life. These single moments were easily forgotten, yet those moments preserved in my scrapbook would not be forgotten and taken for granted. In the process of scrapbooking I learned to tell my story to connect with future generations. The joy of keeping a scrapbook would change the artist in me forever as I stretched and grew in my personal journey.

My memory of a second home was a two story, brick home in the same city—Dallas. From the white frame house, we moved to a traditional multi-colored brick house set on almost one acre of land. Again the address of 8206 Inwood Road ended in an even number. The architect Jon Carsey-designed house stood in the middle of the acre. A long gravel drive on the north side of the house stretched from the three garages to the uncurbed road. The driveway had a concrete walk on the south side running from the house to the road. The mailbox by the road was at the end of the driveway and sidewalk. The lot had trees and Mother planted two small magnolia trees in the front yard. A cedar hedge separated our yard from the neighbors on each side and made us good neighbors.

The house was built when tradition was of value for itself, not as a way of returning from abstract forms that didn't wear well to time's eye. Its scale was a response to humans—warmth and familiarity. The embellishments on the front evolved through past, great periods of architectural history and made us comfortable. The style came from a variety of influences and its simplicity was the complex unity of the touch of a Doric column, New Orleans wrought iron grillwork on a window balcony, a copper front porch roof and near the roof line a tiny half-moon window with a keystone.

The front door opened into a hallway that featured a staircase. A powder room was under the staircase. On the right side of the hall was the living room with a fireplace at the far end. The living room had two doors leading to the family room. On the left side of the hall was the dining room. The dining room led to a small butler's pantry, then to the kitchen which housed a blue leather breakfast table booth. The appliances were modern in that a brick did not have to be added to the oven to keep the temperature even. The kitchen led to the back porch and garage with its washing machine. Upstairs were three bedrooms and two baths. Mother and Daddy converted part of an upstairs, master bedroom deck into a small third bedroom. A third garage was not attached to the house and contained the servants' quarter. A cedar hedge separated the back yard from the service yard.

The front porch was not big enough for socializing or even courting. It was only big enough to stand on to ring the doorbell. We only went in and out the front door to water the front yard. We answered the front doorbell when salesmen called, when we had a party, or when my date would call for me.

The traditional "sitting" porch ended with television. The

inside family room was where we watched the television evening news and soap operas. Backyard patios and swimming pools, in addition to more insular attitudes, killed the idea of a front porch as a social arena for summer months. This time was before security alarms, iron gates, and signs stating "Beware of Dog" and "We Don't Dial 911."

The house had many modern innovations such as central air conditioning. Before air conditioning the relief from the blistering southern heat was the screened porch with a ceiling fan, fans directed over blocks of ice, ice cold lemonade or watermelon, and electric fans blowing across watered down bed sheets.

Air conditioning allowed the South to change the nature of its life. Dallas without air conditioning probably would be just another small town.

In early days the Southern cotton growers had to stay in town for the summer crops and often sent their wives and children to the mountains for the cool air. With families gone, some men would, and could, get in trouble. When air conditioning came the wives and children stayed in town and the moral climate was improved which provided an added benefit of air conditioning.

Another innovation was a dishwasher that was added to the house after we moved. Robert, Morten and I no longer argued about who washed and dried dishes, but whose turn it was to put the dishes in the dishwasher.

In the den we had a player piano that was operated by foot pedals, not electricity. The keys bobbed up and down with an unseen force. We'd sing and act like our fingers were doing the playing, making us "eternal virtuosos." We had a collection of about one hundred player piano rolls. My favorite song was "Who Takes Care of the Caretaker's Daughter While the Caretaker's Busy Taking Care."

The house had a patio adjacent to the den on the back of the house. The patio was curved on the outer edge and bordered by a small knee-high hedge. It was fairly low and there was no danger of falling off. I could easily jump over the hedge to get to the lawn.

The patio provided a place of calm in a busy world. We could imagine a beautiful image in our minds to loosen the grip of a stressful event. It could be a place of tears to cleanse our eyes, souls and mind or provide the emotional release of laughter. Or we could just lower our voices and listen to others. The patio was where our guests were "invited" only, not just those who walked down the street.

We had servants who worked for us. We called them "colored people," which in those days was considered a polite description. On Sundays they would serve breakfast upstairs. One Sunday the family was in Mother and Daddy's bedroom reading the newspapers and visiting. We kept waiting for the maid to come with breakfast. She didn't come. So we went to the servants' quarter to check on her and found that she and her husband had moved out during the night. Mother said, "Colored people don't know how to say goodbye."

Mother and Daddy put a "Dallas Hut" in the far back corner of the yard. The Dallas Hut was the pre-fabricated house that Daddy's company, The Texas Pre-fabricated House and Tent Company, sold during World War II to house the Armed Forces. These huts literally took the Armed Forces out of canvas tents. We painted the hut gray on the outside and our Highland Park High School colors of blue and gold on the inside. There was a piano in the hut and we had lots of parties there. When I was about thirteen years old, sixteen year old Robert had parties there when our parents were not at home. He often had me serve as a "lookout" for when our parents returned home. When I saw my parents coming in the driveway, I blinked the house outside lights. Robert would break up his party and the guests left through the back street. I never tattled on Robert. I imagine that we really didn't fool anyone but ourselves.

The Inwood Road house was the epitome of our family as a unit of five that worked and played together and ate meals together.

But our family unit of five ended on June 11, 1954 when my father died. He was almost forty-eight years old, half a life.

The death of my father who had a manly presence on the side of handsome was a new and fresh experience to all.

Flowers, cards and music did not make his death any easier or cheer us up. We three children were helpless. We were quiet and still as we passed through this dark place. His death reminded us of many dark places such as disappointment, loneliness, and much more. But we knew we must carry on and go forward. His "presence" carried us forward. The path was rough and we dreaded to take this new path, but we did.

My further creative effort was early in my high school and college life when I made an attempt to write in a diary as a way to remember. I didn't name my diaries. I only put my name, address and date on the first page. One page covered a week. I wrote freely in longhand about what happened on a given day. My diary was free of souvenirs such as photographs or flower petals. The day's entry did not end with "Bye" or "Goodnight." But somehow the endeavor stalled. Through the years the diary entries were abandoned and/or lost.

My path ventured into marriage to a young fellow Southern Methodist University (SMU) graduate, Donald Earle Reily who is distinguished looking on the side of handsome. After the death of my father, Mother moved forward with her life. She enrolled in an SMU night course to become an interior designer which was a natural talent. From a chance meeting and a chain of circumstances she met Archie Richard Castleberry from Amarillo, Texas. After a short whirlwind courtship she married Archie who was on the pleasant side of handsome. I was her matron of honor and Don was Archie's best man. Archie cherished the stepfather role as did all of us. Their marriage lasted thirty-one years and I, early on, recognized that Mother was a good judge of men.

My first home with Don was a rambling, white wood frame house in his home town of Corrigan, Texas. It had three acres of Saint Augustine grass in a town of nine hundred people. There were no street names so our address was "the last house in town on United States Highway 287 east to Woodville, Texas." I was as far in the woods as I had ever been. I told Don, "Don't move me any further back into the woods or I will have to hunt to get to town."

A white, wide-plank board fence ran the entire length of the front yard and separated us from the highway. The acreage had a pond in the south front yard, a pond beyond the north side on separate property, and a creek on the east side. The back yard had a patio with an adjacent raised area having a huge spreading oak tree that covered most of the patio and some of the house. Filling out the yard were oak, pine, hickory nut, mimosa, dogwood, redbud, magnolia and pear trees. But there were no pecan trees to leaf out in the spring to signal that winter had ended. The dogwood trees, like a clump of sparkling white next to the tall pines, added a burst of color early each spring in March. There was a rose garden with a concrete border on the driveway side and the roses thrived in the hot afternoon west sun. The entire yard was landscaped with old creosoted railroad ties, Aspidistra or Cast Iron Plant, and Liriope.

The house had been built by Jim Ben Edens who owned Edens-Birth Lumber Company. Every board that went into the construction was examined for perfection before being installed. With an entry hall, very large living room with fireplace, a sizeable dining room, an even larger family room with fireplace and bar area, a galley shaped kitchen and adjoining breakfast room, a long, wide hall connecting to four large bedrooms and baths, we were more than comfortable. The master bedroom and bath had a dressing area housing lots of drawers. I often wondered if I had too many drawers that complicated my life.

The house was not sitting high on piers and beams, as did most Corrigan houses, so you could look through under the house and from the back yard you could see who was standing in the front yard. With no crawl space under the house there was no place for animals to sleep and for any leftover lumber to be stacked. Our house was on a concrete slab with the plumbing, duct work and electrical wiring in the attic.

The driveway bridge over the front pond led from the highway to a two car attached garage which was part of the servants' quarter. Adjacent to this was a service yard with a large 10 x 10 feet dog pen. We didn't have a dog to stay in the pen so we kept our garbage cans in the dog pen to keep the neighbor's dogs from getting into our garbage. A lot of people didn't have a way to keep the neighbor's dogs away so they would put their garbage on the flat-roofed carports. There was no alley or city garbage pickup. A one-arm man collected our garbage. Don suggested I break up any liquor bottles with a hammer before putting them in the garbage. Regardless of how our garbage was hauled off, we became very wasteful when we didn't have to haul it off ourselves.

There was a gravel driveway and I could always hear a car coming up the drive. Eventually, I could recognize a particular person coming by the noise they made as they drove over the wood bridge and gravel. I thought of the curb around the driveway as my "street curb." It was as if I could put my ear to the curb to hear who was coming. From time to time I raked the gravel to fill in the ruts made from the car tires shifting the gravel.

The only thing missing was furniture. We took in any and all furnishings but were cautioned that anything we took from anyone would more than likely remain with us for the remainder of our lives.

Our only television set was in the family room. Our 1960s viewing consisted of *The Flying Nun, Hawaii Five-o, The Farmer's Daughter, Flintstones, Smothers Brothers, Dr. Ben Casey, Dr. Kildare, That Was the Week That Was, That Girl, Laugh In, Carol Burnett Show, Sixty Minutes, Dinah Shore Show, Walt Disney,* and *Perry Como.* We also watched the President John F. Kennedy assassination, and Jack Ruby killing Lee Harvey Oswald.

The house had five doors that we had to check each night to make sure they were locked. Even though we never went out the front door, I always checked it.

We did not have any air conditioning. At night we kept the windows open and the frogs in the pond were so loud I had trouble going to sleep. It sounded like at least a thousand frogs, but if the pond had been drained, it would probably have been only three or four.

Lying in bed late at night with the windows open I could hear the Black folks whistling and singing as they walked out to the colored area called Snow Hill on U. S. Highway 287. The Black culture in Texas was never more evident than when the residents sang on their way home to Snow Hill. This singing of the blues and gospel songs most likely was to keep emotional needs and life styles alive. It was a way of continuing the traditions that evolved out of living close to each other in the same place for long periods of time.

In the back yard we had armadillos, lizards, possums, raccoons, squirrels, salamanders, snakes, rabbits, frogs and crayfish.

The raccoon with his masked face would scurry up a tree after a bird or splash in the pond for a frog. Squirrels had a network in the trees and could travel from one end of the yard to the other without touching the ground. When a lizard crawled in the house, I devised a system of sweeping the lizard with a broom to the door and opening the door for it to run out. The salamanders dug burrows all over the yard. In the fall the Red Spider Lilies popped up in the grass and the raised yard around the patio. The webworms would literally invade the backyard to devour the leaves with their large appetites, leaving a trail of egg-laden webs. The more leaves they ate, the less leaves to rake. They defoliated a tree but did not kill it. When I saw a snake in the yard I called Don at the bank to come kill it. He finally told me, "Nancy, I can't come every time you see a snake." His mother, Julia Belle, gave me a 4/10 shotgun and I learned to kill the snakes myself.

The house constantly had dirt dauber nests (certain kinds of wasps) on the outside. We cleaned them out, but everyone thought they were an asset because dirt daubers kept mosquitoes away.

There was a natural feeling of power that came from subduing and controlling nature.

In our new home in Corrigan I was getting used to being identified as "Don's lady" or the "middle son's wife." I was not well known in Corrigan and was often asked, "Who are you?" I was a newcomer the day I arrived and a newcomer the day I moved ten years later to Lufkin. They meant no harm.

The birth of our two children, Mark Hopkins Reily and Donna Carolyn Reily completed my family. Each child, beautiful in a certain way: Mark on the polished side of handsome; Donna on the warm, effervescent side of beautiful.

With the birth and growth of Mark and Donna I was further lead into creative expression. As my children's activities became more numerous, I began keeping a calendar with their appointments. My first calendar was a small 6 1/2 x 3 3/4 inch green folded promotional, give- away calendar. It was not personalized and would fit into a large shirt pocket. When open it revealed an entire month with no designs, photographs or notations such as full moons or holidays. Soon my monthly calendar became larger and I stapled my notes to it.

A larger calendar was the forerunner to my journal writing. The commitment to write every day with a fountain pen and produce a tangible work signified that I had to get out of my way and let go of the outcome. In other words, grow up and experience life first. The goal was not to express myself, but to communicate which expressed my life's experiences to the present.

Today the primary home of my family, for the third time at an address, 1700 Copeland Street, ending in an even number, is a one story brick building set on a three acre lot in a small town of 35,000, Lufkin, Texas. It's in the Deep East Texas forest at least a thousand miles southeast from Mother's South Fork, Colorado cabin. East Texas is defined as anywhere there is a pine tree.

The facade is a balanced formal look with an eight/twelve

pitch wood shingle roof. A single front door is surrounded with limestone and topped with a limestone keystone. Four shuttered and arched windows define the center of the house. Inside, the floor plan is the standard T-shape hallway design with the living room, dining room, kitchen, four bedrooms and three and one half bathrooms radiating off the hallways. There are no angled walls and entry into the house is only one step at the front door and one step at the back door. As you enter the front door you see that the predominant wall and floor color is a grayish, yellow green that is paler and slightly yellower than average sage green, yellower and lighter than palmetto, and greener and lighter than mermaid—a color called celadon green, nature's background color.

A swimming pool and *cabaña* are added to compliment the two acres of Saint Augustine grass and a third acre retaining all the natural pine trees.

4

The Intervening Years

Although the intervening years brought an expansion of my family, our family is not a "new concept" implying non-core values, but a unique concept of our own within the traditional confines of a "family." It exemplifies the fact that although the number in the family is changing, our human needs remain the same.

Our family is the most fundamental institution that humans require. It's the key social unit where we learn to love, validate our aggressions, develop our conscience and learn values. In today's world our family has great-grandparents, grandparents, parents, children, and encompasses aunts, uncles and cousins. It does take a village. Their primary purpose is to nurture, teach and transmit values and traditions, to be responsible for one another's welfare, and have equal respect for each other's individuality. To nurture is to bring up with care. To teach is to help others learn how to do something. To transmit values and traditions is continuing the ideals, standards, customs and beliefs that our given group regards positively and which shapes our opinions and behaviors.

We are true to ourselves if we care for others' welfare and respect each individual. All this is not as much as togetherness, but as cohesiveness that over the very long haul benefits each. The family unit is not disappearing, but adapting in its role as a strong support system.

With my children as adults, I began the new decade of 1980 keeping a journal instead of a monthly calendar. The first and following journals were 6 x 9 inch. If I traveled for any length of time I took my yearly journal with me. My writing unfolded naturally and when I reviewed the entries, my self-growth was obvious. Hopefully, my journal could be passed down to future generations for insight into my life and times as I attempted to put the truth in the first place rather than second place.

Tuesday, January 1, 1980, South Fork, Colorado—A whole new decade before me. I have been keeping this diary for several years since 1973. Before then I kept a calendar. Even in high school and college I kept diaries. I wish I had kept diaries for every year. I forget where I've been. One thing most notable is the size of the diary page has increased. In high school one page covered a week. Now one page a day and the pages are bigger. Either I've learned more or have more to learn. Things exist in opposites.

Wednesday, December 31, 1980, Houston, Texas—This is not the first day of the year that I've wondered where the time has gone! I can remember how slow time passed as a child. It seemed school days never ended and Christmas and birthdays never got here. The time and motion in an hour glass passed so slowly. But now time sifts through so quickly and I'm making as fast of tracks as I can to keep up with the motion. I'll bring 1980 to a close before I get to the next page of the 1980 diary which is titled, "Earnings and Withholding Tax." Happy 1981.

Thursday, January 1, 1981, Lufkin, Texas—A beautiful, crisp, sunny day. What a beginning! I got to laughing over so many things we have done and that our calendar is already filling up at least until June. Just because I start a new diary today doesn't mean I start from scratch. I bring the last few months and years with me!

Thursday, December 31, 1981, Lufkin, Texas—I read out loud pages of my 1981 diary. Don said it just wore him out listening. I told him, "We haven't even gotten to the busy part." He sighed.

Mark brought into our family Jane Read, who is on the sophisticated side of beautiful.

He met her in the eighth grade, so we always thought of her as part of our family. Their love for each other was a choice. The two wanted love and felt they deserved it as they surrendered their egos to something bigger than themselves.

For the wedding rehearsal dinner, Mark wanted the gathering held at our house. I declared it a seated dinner for the one hundred guests. We constructed a garden room out of the two-car garage by nailing panels to the garage door openings, installed two window air conditioning units, placed plants around the room which built to a focal point of two white Grecian urns and candelabras on the garage door wall. Green carpet lined the floor.

We set four tables in the garage/garden room, places for twelve in the dining room decorated with garlands of white flowers— enough to catch my breath, and seated eight in the breakfast room.

All the furniture in the den was placed in a rental truck. Six tables were set up in the den for guests. Coral and yellow flowers with Tropicana roses added the finishing touches.

During the evening Mark and I were standing alone in the front hall as the violinist serenaded the group and strolled by us. Mark began trying to thank me and tears came to his eyes. I told him I knew what he was trying to say and that I knew it was all there. Just don't say it now or I'll dissolve into tears. We hugged and joined the party.

At the wedding rehearsal dinner in the dining room Mark toasted his future bride, "I met my love in the eighth grade at a church party playing 'Spin the Bottle' and I knew then she was special." My college graduate son continued his toast to his college graduate fiancé through his teary voice. No one had a dry eye in the room or could make a toast after his! Afterwards, all the guests gathered in the back yard and toasted the couple.

About midnight we started dismantling the den and Don went out to the rental truck, returned and in a calm tone of voice said, "I can't get the padlock off the truck." I told him that the padlock had to come off because I wanted to have the house in order for Mark's wedding day. After much WD 40, off came the padlock, the den was put back in order and the dirty rental dishes stacked in the rental truck.

On Mark's wedding day he seemed calm but on another wave length. He was quiet, reserved, noticing everything and very appreciative of all the activity. He didn't want to see his bride-to-be on their wedding day.

By mid-afternoon my family gathered to start dressing for the 4:00 pm wedding. My daughter, Donna, was a bridesmaid in a coral blouse with a white moire, ankle length skirt with flowers hand painted on the bottom, and a turquoise sash. Don and Mark were in oxford gray formal attire—striped trouser, light gray vest, white winged collar, striped ascot and gray coat.

Our maid, Mary Griffin, and I had rehearsed getting me dressed in my beige chiffon dress with a matching scarf to trail down the back. I was told by others and I agreed to wear beige and be quiet which I did to bring calmness to my son's day.

The church sanctuary was full and I had expected to get teary eyed, but an emotion came over me that I had never felt before. It was a level so high I didn't want it to end.

Mark and Jane said their vows promising to love, honor, cherish and obey with the basic expectation that people do what they say they are going to do. If they say these things and don't mean them, then it was a serious delinquency. Love includes accepting all the idiosyncrasies, honor means fidelity which creates a bond of commitment publicly declared in the wedding ceremony, cherish is to hold dear, and obey means having your spouse nudge you in the right direction. It's just the law of survival to stay together with teamwork with all the love, honor, cherish, and obey to create oneness that so many want to experience. The cult of the individual should not undermine the institution of marriage. The Golden Rule was their motto—to teach it by example with integrity.

The minister pronounced them husband and wife, they kissed and walked quickly up the aisle. It was their moment. What a fun time. I've just never had a better time. I've gained a special daughter and the arena enlarged. Hopefully, they will always "count their blessings" rather than "nurse their grievances."

Our prince married his princess and Don gave me a book,

Invitation to A Royal Wedding, by Kathryn Spink. Princess Diana and Prince Charles of England had married the same year, only two days before Jane and Mark. Don inscribed the book:

> My dear Nancy, Diana and I are sorry you could not attend our wedding, but certainly understand with all of your own wedding festivities taking place at the same time. Please accept this book as a memento of the occasion. When your bride and groom's wedding book is published we would love to have a copy. Sincerely, Charles, P.W.

January 1, 1982, Lufkin, Texas—Don brought me in this red 1982 journal several weeks ago. I am pleased as it's a larger page and I'm beginning to need more space. I started out several years ago with a half page for each day. No telling where I'll be in three or four years as to page size. Today is the beginning of a new year—the beginning of firsts when I reconcile the lasts with the firsts.

December 31, 1982, Dallas, Texas—Don and I spent New Year's Eve at the Fairmont Hotel in Dallas with a seven course dinner and hearing Frank Sinatra, Jr. If his father was not such a recognizable name, you would never think to compare him with anyone. His voice and presence stands by itself. A perfectly delightful evening and a beautiful way to close 1982, a year of recession and great unemployment. I don't think anyone will miss 1982.

Saturday, January 1, 1983, Dallas, Texas—Yesterday I

wrote of my day and of a brief look backward. Today I write of my day and of a look forward. I continue writing in my journal as a gift to myself, as a way to remind me of my true worth, as a centering point in my life, and as a conversation with myself telling the stories of my life. I recall reading some of my mother's journals and treasure her outlook. I begin this year with renewed hope.

Saturday, December 31, 1983, Dallas, Texas—Don started back actively in real estate. He's so much happier working and my house is much cleaner to him! It's exciting to see him producing because he's so happy. Work is best for us all, it's mankind's central theme.

It was almost one year to the day of Jane and Mark's 1981 wedding when our routine day ended. We went to bed early and at 2:30 am Donna, our college graduate daughter, called that she and her college sweetheart, Ray Archer Davis, who was on the friendly side of handsome, were going to drive to Lufkin. They drove in and rang the doorbell. Ray, with a controlled facial and body language, stayed outside on the front porch and said that he and Donna wanted to get married and would like our blessing. What we had anticipated had happened. Our future son-in-law had a loose diamond in his blue jean pocket. The next day they had the diamond mounted in a platinum setting.

All the myriad details for a daughter's wedding were put in motion—reserving the church and country club, invitations, the wedding dress, the bridesmaid dresses, the bridesmaid gifts, newspaper articles, addressing twelve hundred invitations, cake tasting, rice bags, displaying gifts, hotel reservations for guests—all designed to take my mind off that fact that Donna was "marrying and leaving home."

The rehearsal dinner toasts included the only advice my mother gave me when I married: "To Donna, Don't ever put your hand on the lawnmower." I added that I would share Donna with Ray. His toast to the most beautiful girl in the room ended the toasts on a high level.

At the wedding I wore beaded colors to blend with the burgundy bridesmaid dresses. Donna looked breathtakingly beautiful as she and her father walked down the aisle. She was on her father's right arm and he held her left fingertips with his other hand. I could feel their emotion as my daughter had a faint smile and her father looked solemn.

Their wedding vows included to love, honor, cherish, and obey, the same as Jane and Mark's wedding. After being pronounced husband and wife, they didn't need to kiss their mothers and fathers "goodbye" as they started down the aisle, because that was all understood. They were on the path to speak the truth, break bread together, get rid of the lust in each life, master flexibility, and believe in some solitude. The path backed up with commitment. The mask protecting boundaries of space would be unmasked for survival. Each would take on the burden of each other's life, but couldn't put either on hold. Each assumes personal responsibilities of thoughts, words, attitudes, and actions—which receive reward or punishment.

I anticipate the arrival of my first grandchild given to us in 1983 by Jane and Mark. I pass the time by nervously cleaning out the accumulation of possessions in the attic, the captured photographs of long ago relatives, and our boxes of heartfelt childhood mementoes. Both my children have homes now so I can pass their possessions to them or throw them away. Then with a further delay in the birth, I clean closets, cabinets, and put my house in order for the six of us, soon to be more. By now I only hear half of what people tell me.

The minute I become a grandmother I am bestowed with certain characteristics such as bragging rights and an intense impulse to be equal to the favorite grandparent. I learn not to prophesy unless I know.

From the day I am told that I am going to be a grandmother I am glad that I am not asked what to name the baby. I am permitted to request what I am called. Some decide on cultural traditions, some by themselves and some by toddler phonetic repetition. I know my first born grandchild will not call me anything for a while and when the baby does say my name it will be garbled. But I am willing to wait not to be called "Mom's mom," "Granny" or the like, but to be renamed Grandmother which is what I want to be called because that's what I called my Grandmother. She was among the last of grandmothers who daily unwound their long hair. She did not deny her age which would have led to an unwanted second childhood. My hair is short and I don't look like my Grandmother.

Jane, if she feels like during her pregnancy that her first born claims all of her body and thoughts, and that she isn't sure if her life is her own, she never sheds a tear.

A telephone call from Mark informs us that Jane is near birthing our first grandchild. With Mark by her side, not cowering behind the swinging doors of the delivery room, a grandson is brought into the family. I have never seen a bigger smile on Mark's face as he came out of the delivery room with a Polaroid photograph of his first born. I feel the joy in his heart as my son is being called on to further his role of protector. This child is called Read Hopkins

Reily after his mother's maiden name and my maiden name which is Mark's middle name. Read will grow to be on the masculine, classy side of handsome.

When I see my beautiful daughter-in-law, Jane, she is beside herself with happiness. When I see my first grandson he is unblemished, has long fingers, and favors his mother in his looks. His eyes are not a cerulean blue but a smoky gray-blue. They will stay blue to be my only blue-eyed grandchild. That first night my son sleeps on the hospital floor to be near the new mother.

We don't know how many brothers and sisters our first grandchild will have, but he will be the only child to know the others from their birth. We will not spoil him, only with love.

No matter what we expect we are not prepared. Don and I are officially grandparents. We have come full circle. We are given a gift, a present not to be neglected. Our first grandchild gives us awareness that life is to be lived in the present. The grandparent-grandchild bond is second only to the parent-child bond. Grandparents provide the connection between generations. We tie them to their roots. As active grandparents my grandchildren will see us before the faded, yellowed, photographs in the family albums. These albums in the attic are full of treasures. Besides, we offer cushions for stress and a safe harbor.

We fall in love with our first grandson. We are making the grand passage with no classes or counseling on how to love. It's a pure love that can never hurt us. We want Read to know how special he is and hope we are special to him. All we have to do is be present as we watch our children do things right.

My first time to be a grandparent comes easily although my age group playfully wants to burn the American Association of Retired Persons (AARP) cards. It enables me to lose my ridiculous sense of self-importance that occurred when I gave birth to my children. But it returned when my children left home. Becoming a grandparent encourages me to forget about myself as quickly as becoming a parent. I am not nonchalant about Read's birth and envision not being nonchalant about the practice of manners. With his coming gift of the English language by using different words than the masses, Read shows signs of class. His optimism soothes the uncertainties of life from becoming overpowering.

I hesitate to tell Mark that raising a child has peaks and valleys and that one thing is constant, the love for the child, an overwhelming love he has never before felt. Babies can handle all the love you can give them. They put no obstacles in your way to let you love them.

I then add to the back of my Monte Cristo hat a pin made of a silver concho measuring 3 1/4 x 2 3/4 inch with a turquoise in the center of the design. The pin anchors the hat for a good fit and will keep the wind from blowing it off.

With everyone still in the hospital, four days later, a telephone call from Dallas by Mark, "Please come, we need you." I quickly responded to the call and that first night and several days later, I sleep in the room with my first born grandchild.

Standing by his crib, like I am waiting for a baby to become a child, is the secret part of grandmothering. Jane, Mark and I want to get things running smoothly that first day, but soon realize Read is in charge of our schedule. Read reminds me of the advantages of patience and time management.

As Jane and Mark start to bathe Read for the first time in the kitchen sink, they stand back very shyly. I say, "Sooner or later you will have to touch him, he won't break." Afterwards, Read eats, cuddles on our shoulders, sleeps, and cries ever so softly when he needs us.

When the schedule runs smoothly, Jane and Mark, under my

advisement, make a car trip of only forty-five minutes because I have no "dinner baskets."

I am officially a grandmother as one to become more closely involved in my grandchildren's lives as an economic and emotional support without a million speeches.

In a few months for Read's christening, it takes his mother and father, and both his grandmothers to get him dressed in the same white suit that Mark wore for a baby photograph. Everyone settles down when we enter Dallas' Highland Park Presbyterian Church sanctuary and are seated in the front pews. Read is good during the ceremony and takes it all in only to give a cry when the minister's big hand wet with water touches the top of his head.

As our first grandchild, we take nothing for granted in his development. Elation when my blue-eyed Read first turns over, takes his first crawling steps, clings to his mother and father but warms up to his grandparents quickly, touching everything, sitting in the same high chair as my two children did much earlier and playing in a red wagon at Christmas time.

Then the unexpected happens when Read has surgery at eight months. Most of us think the world is predictable, fair and understandable.

But we can't prepare for everything because all our lives are of unforeseen events. Read responds to events in life as only a young child with miraculous resiliency. Crawling everywhere, standing without holding on, picking up things with two fingers instead of his whole hand. Taking steps holding on, then taking seven or eight steps, losing his balance, falling and crawling the rest of the way. Saying a few isolated words, climbing up and down the stairs, Read keeps track of a big twelve inch plastic ball, and says "ball" over and over.

At Read's first birthday we celebrate with a party. He says lots of words and babbles as he walks steadily. He is still saying "ball."

Jane and Mark take their first vacation away from him and upon their return five days later Read weeps when he sees them. Five days is a long time in the life of a one year old.

Our first grandchild is climbing all over boxes, saying two syllable words such as balloon, hello, ice tea, and finally looks at me and says, "Grandmother." I have waited for Read to call me Grandmother because I know any other grandchildren will follow his lead. He produces for me and if you divide the word into grand and mother, how can I lose. There are two times in life when I get a new name: once when born and once when a grandmother.

Read is more interested in action than words. I am often on the floor with him playing ball as a playmate. We just want to have fun, play for the sake of play, and get lost in the moment. I am being "grandmothered in."

A ray of sunshine appeared as Read understands most of what one says. When at our house, full of energy he comes to my bedside about 9:00 pm and says "book." I read his book to him and he plays under our silk bed sheets and bed covers. Because his mother is attempting to get him to stop taking a bottle, he comes out of the sheets and announces, "No more bottles." I see the world the way he sees it.

When in school Read receives an award for "problem solving." At eight years of age Read is playing baseball and says, "I want to go to church in the morning although it gives me a headache and I don't understand a word he says."

Years later when Read is working in a job as a restaurant waiter, he is "taken back" with a woman customer's meanness. The incident makes him think of us as not being bitter. My twenty-three year Read calls to tell us what kind and good grandparents we are. Tears come to my eyes.

As our family grows it becomes more obvious that my mother and stepfather's cabin in the Rocky Mountains is not large enough to accommodate our increasing families of Robert, Morten and me.

We start "walking the land" in the Rocky Mountains which are a showcase of over mile-high peaks, ridges, meadows and valleys. From the Great Plains west they reach Alaska to end south of Santa Fe. Just a few hundred miles north of Santa Fe is the San Luis Valley between two ranges of the Rocky Mountains. Adjacent to the San Luis Valley is the Rio Grande National Forest. In this western edge of the San Luis Valley geological events over millions of years ago resulted in two rapid rivers converging—the South Fork of the Rio Grande into the Rio Grande to become the third largest river in the United States, but not the most crooked.

To find the site for our future cabin we walk zigzag on Elk Creek Ranch property adjacent to the Rio Grande National Forest. We are not wandering aimlessly in circles. We walk a clear path void of spring muds and pussy willow blooms to discover and act upon our endeavor.

I prepare for the day by admitting I am vain. I have a more-than-normal pride in how I look. I am not obsessed, only to look my best at this age. The night cleansing cream is removed with a cotton CleanSoft facial cloth. I apply a light foundation make-up color to match my natural colored skin. Although one is considered of the working class in earlier days if your skin is tanned, I have a slight tan from the sun and today I am of a refined upper class.

I am not sure I need a hat, but I take one and debate whether to give in to the urge to go with my decorative urge by placing a hat on my head.

My shirt is the traditional style with a collar, sleeves with cuffs and a full vertical opening with buttons. It has a long tail to encourage me to tuck it in. There are no frills at the neck or cuffs and the blue color, which is still Crayola's most popular color, is considered casual wear.

My activity does not require the rugged, heavy thread, safety stitching and sturdy metal zippers in my denim cotton slacks. But I do not know what the day will bring.

My hand pulls a handkerchief out of my slacks which is a far cry from the common use of a handkerchief in ancient Greece some 2,000 years before. Our notion of a handkerchief came into general use during the time of 1200–1500 A.D., otherwise known as the Renaissance. Today my handkerchief is square, defying the round shape and is intended for "show and blow."

My leather walking shoes have fine hand stitching. The light weight cork and latex construction creates a firm walking surface that is shock absorbent and durable. I am not sure I can erase all the dressing rules for this path, so I don't dress up my shoes for walking.

My wrist watch has a blue leather band and a wind-up stem. It doesn't depend on the movement of my arm only or a daily winding to keep the minute and hour hand in correct time. It brightens reality, refreshes my memory, gives me guidance and shows antiquity. It doesn't show beneath my long sleeves buttoned at the wrist. It's certainly not a diminutive-in-scale cocktail watch with diamonds.

We walk up and down the road from Mother's cabin looking at all the possible sites. It is just the beginning of the process. We don't need a map. What do we want, what site do we like, what can we afford, what does the family like? We don't want to be by the highway or by the big lake. We want a view. Lots of decisions, but they are our decisions.

Even before I began journal entries for 1984 I made a list, "Goals for 1984." It was better than just thinking about them. When I wrote them I didn't care about spelling, punctuation, or editing them. It was a way of parking my concrete short-term and long-term goals. With all that was going on, it kept me on track. I had interests that resulted in several projects at one time because I'd get one going and come to a stumbling block in time or research. This way I kept moving on one of my projects such as my memoirs, photography handbook, and photography.

January 1, 1984, Dallas, Texas—This is the year George Orwell wrote about, 1984, and everyone is making quite a fuss over it. He warned against the dangers of a totalitarian society and abusive authority. It was not his prophecy, but today's writers are making it such. My journal this year is even bigger than last year. It makes it easier to write in with the pages so big. The need is not as it seems, just that I cannot find one the same size as last year's book. There is an air of optimism around everywhere such as unemployment is dropping, inflation holding steady at a point lower than previous years, and only scant talk of rising interest rates.

Monday, December 31, 1984, Dallas, Texas—The day started off with a few light snow flurries. It's fun to reminisce about the past year. I made a list of goals for 1984 and I met some of them and plan to continue with them in 1985. I think my 1984 list was more for five years than three, so my list for 1985 will be an adaptation and continuance of 1984. Don and I commented that we didn't feel in control of our lives this year, but laughingly said that might be the best thing. I close with a grateful heart.

It was unexpected, but when our family increased by one person, we lost one in 1984 in the logical order of life. As if it was planned, as our family increased, death decreased the family. My Aunt Helen who was on the aristocratic side of beautiful and Uncle Winfield Morten who was a true gentleman on the side of handsome had for years introduced me to a New Mexico land where nature's spectacular gift was all the colors on all color charts. The sights always fascinated me and I listened to the land. The days there were full of passionate action which related to happiness. Uncle Winfield had died in 1968 at age sixty-four after a courageous battle from cancer. Things changed for Aunt Helen and from the wisdom of insecurity she reinvented herself. Aunt Helen was now in her eighties and had a right to know of death which might bring more illumination.

For Aunt Helen age was a matter of mind. She didn't want her age known, but it didn't matter to me. If the age barrier was based on illness and being needed, she broke the barrier by being healthy and fulfilled.

Finally, a stroke silenced my dear, courageous Aunt Helen. I visited her and when I looked at her and the stories her face could tell, I didn't see age, but just saw her. With her left side paralyzed, her expression never changed. As I left that day I told her I'd see her later. She barely parted her lips and it sounded like, "bye." Somehow I felt like it was the final "goodbye." Death comes similar to the birth of a baby, when it's time.

Each person approaches his death in his own unique way. She lived a colorful, grateful life and didn't want to take years to separate from her physical body. My Aunt Helen must have recognized the shift within her person which took her from a mental processing of death to a realistic belief in her own mortality. She was more ready to die than I was to lose her. She simply withdrew from everything outside of herself and went "inside" where there was only room for her. With more sleep time, she was preparing for the important work of dying which is a private level of which outsiders were not aware. Words were not as important, but touch and wordlessness meant more. With less and less appetite for food, her energy was from a spiritual source. As sleep increased, she seemed to have one foot in each world until the final step into her new life.

After my visit, a few days later, at eighty-four years of age, Aunt Helen's lungs filled with fluid and she just quit breathing. To me the worst part of her passing was that there will never be another Aunt Helen.

We buried Aunt Helen next to Uncle Winfield with the dates of her birth and death (1900–1984). We recalled the days that meant the most—the days represented by the dash between the dates when she had her first smile, first steps, first friends, first love and many firsts until when it was time for the last goodbye.

Tuesday, January 1, 1985, Dallas, Texas—The New Year begins and George Orwell's *1984* probably should be re-read to see what came true because television attempted to manipulate us. I'm making a list for 1985 of my goals. I find it very interesting to do and take it with a grain of salt.

Tuesday, December 31, 1985, Dallas, Texas—Don and I celebrated New Year's Eve with friends, dinner, dancing and fireworks. My children will be proud of me because I stayed up until 2:00 am. We've had good and bad this year. I am very blessed with a loving family.

An early morning event brings my second grandchild, a grandson to join the family. No matter how many grandchildren I have, there is a certain excitable tension that accompanies a baby's arrival. He is given the name of Thomas Donald Reily. Thomas is a name Jane and Mark like and Donald is the name of his fraternal grandfather. He captures all our hearts with beautiful dark brown eyes and very dark brown hair. Thomas is on the photogenic side of handsome.

I add another turquoise and silver pin with a 1 1/2 x 1 1/2 inch five point design to my Monte Cristo hat. The pin's center holds eight stones with one in the center and the five points radiate outward with each holding various amounts of three to five stones.

As our second grandchild, we begin building a relationship based on true affection. It's easy to listen to Thomas and ask him questions and sit back and let him know he is being heard. To not sound like parents, we offer little advice and become a special confidant.

We take Read to see Thomas at the hospital in Lufkin. On the way we eat lunch in the breakfast room at our house. Among other items, cottage cheese is served. Mark asks Read to take a bite of the cottage cheese. Read eats a bite and says, "It doesn't taste like candy." On the way to the hospital Read says, "They don't have a baby hippopotamus at the hospital." Read adjusts beautifully to having a baby brother.

We are grandparents for a second time with some experience. Again, we are given a gift, a present. Thomas gives us an awareness that life is to be lived each day as it comes. He teaches us not to neglect his gift and don't be fazed when anything doesn't go as planned. He grows stronger and stronger under the support system of a family that mentors.

He reminds us that our natural breaking down of the body and the natural cycle of change as our vision blurs and peers into the distant past, renders some of the contemporary world as absurd. This is to be faced, not hidden away. All this comes from an inner strength on Thomas' and our part because he knows where he stands and that we are there for him. He helps us to slow down the pace of our life so we can learn from him. His intelligence is expressed in visual images. Thomas is mellow in his mannerisms, very affectionate and always has a smile. His coming good manners put people at ease because he presents himself appropriately which is the best qualification for eloquence. In his childhood, he discovers courage, knowledge and heart.

Don and I had a slight introduction into the "sandwich generation" of caring for parents, children and grandchildren when his father, Gordon Clinton Reily, who was on the inclusive side of handsome, was diagnosed with Parkinson's Disease. With his mother, Julia Belle Reily who was on the happy side oof beautiful, able to care for him, we were only involved as helpers to her. When he developed pneumonia he had to be hospitalized. His congestive heart failure worsened and his lungs filled with fluid. Not able to overcome all his frailties, he died peacefully in 1977. Afterwards, Don and his brother, Mickey, talked to Julia Belle about having someone live with her. She ushered them out of the house and told me later, "Don and Mickey are the two bossiest farts I know." This was our first attempt in the sandwich generation.

But by the early 1980s Don and I were officially the sandwich generation. Being almost the first of the sandwich generation was a learning process by my generation as the previous generations "knew it all." This rather confirmed what I had felt and knew. I related to these two generations, one before me, the other after me, but I was not of them and not responsible for their actions, although I felt a sense of protection for the older generation, but I couldn't protect them from themselves, only from outside forces. I spent a fair amount of time following behind my parents "picking up the pieces."

The world was changing and I was inundated with things of the past that no longer applied. Mother began talking to me about her moving to Lufkin. She talked to me about it, but wasn't quite ready. She was getting ready to move on. She asked me to not abandon her and Archie. I told her I wouldn't. She was not alone and I was not alone.

Mother started growing old in other people's eyes, then she slowly realized their judgment. Mother was aging and the category was young-old, not old-old or oldest-old. She was still on the engaging side of beautiful. She was still vibrant and fun, but conscious of aging as inevitable, but deemed as a waste of everyone's time. She had witnessed her inner growth as not a given, but worked diligently to arrive at spiritual aging although she still had desires, passions, loves, and irritations. She had lots of stories in her face, and I realized she was a repository of wisdom. She was the real thing. Her exit strategy was piling up as she learned many of her friends had died.

I knew one of these days I would have to give up Mother. I didn't want to but I knew I would have to. She talked to me briefly about how we had to give up our loved ones. We have been a good mother and daughter and no one will ever take her place. Even in her fragile condition, I lean on her and learn from her.

When I took Mother to her first retirement apartment, she said, "This isn't my favorite thing to do." I replied, "I know, but I am walking with you." Many years later as Mother gave her possessions to family, she commented, "It's an end of an era and I feel like the end is nearer." She lived nine more years.

Caregivers in the sandwich generation function best when everyone else is in crisis. One day Mother got aggravated at herself. I gave her a pep talk on her attitude because now I was the parent. The next day when I walked into her room she greeted me with a smile and said, "How do you like my smiling face?" We hugged.

Don would often say about our sandwich position, "We haven't had anyone call us at the 'Crisis Center today.'" We can't help everyone but we can listen.

Once when we got ready to go to the cabin without Mother, I told her, "I hate to leave you." She replied, "I left you at times." She wrote us a loving note to enjoy her cabin.

The sandwich generation again surfaced when Read and Thomas joined Mother, Don and me for hamburgers. When we sat at the table, Thomas asked, "Has everyone been served." His comment was not unexpected, but it expanded our horizons. Then when we started eating, my Read said, "I'm waiting for the blessing." Mother said the blessing.

When the telephone rings at our house early one 1985 morning and Don opens the bedroom hall door hurriedly, I know that it is about Donna giving birth to a grandchild in the hospital in Corpus Christi, Texas, a city six hours away. With my check-list in hand, I gather everything I will need for the event.

I am given a warning of becoming a grandmother to my daughter's child. I think I know, but I am not prepared. When I arrive in mid-afternoon in her city, I can't go see Donna for my heart being in my throat will cause tears. I am not that brave. I know I will burst into tears, not a simple cry, but a cry that brings memories of everyone who comes before me: my father who died before I married, my grandparents whom some I knew, aunts, uncles and I progress to my mother giving birth to me, and my giving birth to Donna, and the ultimate sense of all belonging to each other. Many years later Donna told me that I didn't have to brave everyday.

It is a link-feeling when your beautiful daughter gives birth to her child, a feeling of oneness with Donna. I am the first one to hear Donna's heartbeat. Not so much a sacrifice, but a gift.

While I wait in the waiting room, hoping Donna will understand, with "tongue in cheek" I send word that she can deliver now that her mother is here! Shortly afterwards Ray rolls Donna and new granddaughter out of the delivery room and says, "Would you believe a girl."

Carolyn Frances Davis, our first granddaughter, is given my middle name, Carolyn, and Frances, a name her parents like. She is our third grandchild and I am an even more patient grandmother. Carolyn is on the appealing side of beautiful.

About this time I add to my Monte Cristo hat a third turquoise and silver pin measuring 3 x 2 1/2 inch in the shape of a butterfly. The butterfly's wings are ribbed and hinged with a turquoise stone in the middle of the hinge.

Meanwhile, at the hospital we hold Carolyn to make photographs and retreat to our hotel room overlooking the bay. After a few days, I decide to leave and allow the new parents to handle their daughter. But Donna asks me to stay close by in a hotel for one more night because as they stand for the first time in front of their daughter on the changing table, I tell them, "Sooner or later you will have to touch her. She won't break."

Now we are grandparents for the third time and given a gift, a present—that with a child, it is a compromise between military discipline and laissez-faire flexibility. Donna and Ray will offer a firm base to manage the peaks and valleys and we will keep the family values alive in a non-threatening way as we adopt the role of "fumblers."

When Carolyn was little, she was shy and timid. She was afraid of Chuck E. Cheese. At her first and only ballet recital rehearsal, she cried and only performed after a promise of seeing the *Little Mermaid* video.

We talk to Carolyn about her favorite things to share so when she thinks of her favorite things, she will associate them with us.

In time at grandparents' day at her school I will sit in those small chairs with my chin on my knees and my back in distress as she explains her latest school project. The event sharpens my listening skills. Carolyn asks me, "Are you old?" I answer, "Compared to what?"

Carolyn knows that good manners and good sense go together. With her good manners and a zest for living, she will always be welcome by putting people at ease. She is not afraid to have fun with a chance I may laugh with her. Carolyn can handle all the love we can give her. She puts no obstacles in our way to let us love her.

Although far away in distance, I stay in touch with Carolyn with large-print letters and birthday cards. Later with phone calls, e-mails, and text messages in late night or early morning.

I send photographs to all my grandchildren when they are quite young, so they will remember us. Their photographs remind me that I can sense all the love in those small faces. When the grandchildren are little and visit us, I always have a toy on their bed when they arrive.

When a couple of Carolyn's elementary school classmates are

placed in an advanced class, her mother asks her, "Do you mind not being in that class?" Carolyn says, "No, because the cute boys are in my class."

Carolyn's shyness subsides and her inherited organization characteristics from her mother, grandmother and great-grand-mother later come forth as she travels to the cabin and gives each of her guests an itemized list for grocery shopping for the week's menu.

My parent's cabin is full and overflowing. I welcome the opportunity to leave and begin a new tradition. I share the event with Don because after all these years my head and heart still know he is my friend. Our marriage survives ecstasy, misery and tolerance. That we have survived because we know that to love your spouse "forever" does not mean "for as long as it makes you happy or until your spouse fails to meet your expectations."

The day begins as I make myself presentable to myself and others. I add moisturizer and a barrier cream for environmental irritants. Then I smooth on my basic foundation make-up. The skin challenges are in years to come.

My Monte Cristo hat is laden with three turquoise pins, but not enough to weigh it down to escape being blown off by the wind. I tighten the shoe lace string under my chin.

If I am not hiking in the forest, I could pair a silk shirt with my blue jeans. But for practical purposes and appealing to everyone, I put on a T-shirt with no collar or buttons and made of stretchy, finely knit cotton with short sleeves. There is no designer insignia, advertisement or "bumper sticker like saying." It is not even in the color of the year. The wearing depends on my physique.

I dress for the occasion in my easy fit but not loose-fit, five-pocket light colored blue jeans where the actual measurements match those on the label. The pre-washed jeans have no shredded knees and frayed hems.

My handkerchief in my hip pocket is folded into a four-square-inch square to easily fit my hip contour without bulging the fabric. The layout of this vintage, multi-color hankie as documented in Helen Gustafson's *Hanky Panky, An Intimate History of the Handkerchief,* is a far cry from floral designs, but contains small calorie counting squares with the square caloric count for "Bon-Bons, Danger."

My hiking shoes are the best blend of comfort and performance. They allow my muscles to function efficiently to suffer less fatigue.

To tell the time, I don't have to rely on the shadows cast by the sun because I have a wrist watch showing the hour, minute, day and date. It is not a piece of jewelry, but an all-weather, stainless steel time piece surrounded by a blue, enamel-like band to compliment the blue leather band. In the daytime I can read it easily because of its size. Time devours everything.

I don't have to call "shotgun" as the two of us climb into my mother's old Jeep Wagoneer to again ride the roads searching for a cabin building site. We want a view because at home the tall, stately pines of our primary home means we miss the views of the clouds, sunrises and sunsets. We want to see the low humidity clouds peeking over the mountain ridge each day, each hour, as they reinvent the sky. The clouds bombard the sunrises and sunsets to show us the qualities of light and air as they interact on the landscape. We still want a site not too close to the highway to avoid the automobile lights and not too close to the Rio Grande. We are not addicted to noise and don't want any noise such as the automobiles and the river noise. The absence of noise is the absence of aural graffiti.

We climb out of the Jeep and walk the land looking for building sites. I walk up an incline full of aspen, spruce and pine. Finally we find a small clearing of sandy soil half way up a mountain in a canyon. We choose a site not too high on the mountain so our Jeep can make the uphill grade; nor too rocky to provide water. The view doesn't disappoint us as it expands in three directions and includes the rocky formation we call "Lady Fingers." So named because of the description we give the grids of divided vertical, rectangular rocks that resemble a baked Lady Finger cake.

We agree on the site. Don asks me if I select this site to be close to Mother's cabin. I reply, "It never enters my mind until you mention it." Don walks the land finding the corners that zigzag through our community land at Elk Creek Ranch and the United States Rio Grande National Forest.

We acquire a plat of the ranch's land at the county court house to pinpoint our site. We allow a passage of time to know if we have chosen the right building site. Our dreams are put on hold while autumn and winter settle the earth for the following spring groundbreaking of our creation.

5

A Creative Life

I was thirty-nine years old when I drove Donna and her best friend, Harriet Duncan, to Mother's cabin. After our arrival the girls were busy learning to drive the Scout. I stretched out on Mother's bed one day with a yellow legal tablet and began making notes—"When I come to the mountains, I always gain perspective." Prompting me to do this was a writer's great "sense of place." As I wrote I could hear Donna and Harriet gunning the Scout to eventually hang it on a big rock.

My cosmetics then had a prominent place in my day's routine. My foundation make-up included moisturizer, advanced cream, and a light texture eye saving cream to support the eye area and its first signs of fine lines.

My then unadorned hat resided nearby on the dresser.

My blue and white striped shirt of one hundred percent cotton looked good with its high quality of construction. Its long sleeves covered my watch. Whatever my activity the shirt would withstand years of use and would actually look better with the passage of time. It had a pocket for my pen and note paper.

I was dressed in my blue jeans, not the white ones that are high fashion, because the blue ones were more adaptable. With easily more than two hundred brand names of jeans, each fit differently. Sometimes it took trying on at least sixteen different styles for the perfect fit, an easy fit, and certainly not a custom fit.

My man-size handkerchief resided in my front left hand blue jeans pocket. Machine hemmed with no embroidered initials, its use varied from cleaning my glasses to tending to my other needs.

My shoes were more for walking than hiking.

My watch indicated that in our culture the use of my time in an efficient, productive way was a "high art." There was no hidden button when pressed to reveal the time. As the pace of my life went faster, my definition of a moment was shorter and shorter. My awareness of time unfolded into more minute increments forced me to leave no time to experiment with an event in a meaningful way.

As the day ended, I knew I was in a visually empowering landscape. It would be easy to lie down at night and close my eyes with the landscape images parading on the inside of my eyelids. It was then easy to recognize that seeing became before words— seeing that established my sense of place.

I kept making notes for several years with no vision of where the note writing was taking me. When I had four yellow tablets full of handwritten notes that didn't even have doodle marks in the margin, I couldn't throw them away. I wanted to do something with them. I'd always loved reading *Gift from the Sea* by Anne Morrow Lindbergh who wrote of her life's experiences using the sea as the background. I decided to write of my life's experiences set in the mountains.

Twelve years later, by myself in a rectangular of quiet at my mother's cabin, I was ready to carve this private space for my writing life. How fortunate, indeed, that I had choices. I purposely worked at a table not facing a wall, but with a view, to manage the contest between writing and non-writing. The contest was within the writing as it widened and deepened. In my early days of writing, I needed encouragement and received little. I rarely showed my manuscript except to my editor.

Now that I wrote and knew creating was a skill and that to create was to be reborn, I didn't need the encouragement from others so much and was beginning to receive encouragement. I knew where I was in regard to my level of writing. I often thought I was more a researcher and organizer than a writer.

My interest in purposeful writing actually began with reading. One of my first recollections was Mother, who was a reader, taking me to the small Austin stone building trimmed with limestone known as the Lakewood Branch of the Dallas Public Library. On each side of the wooden double doors was an open book sculptured in low relief limestone. As I entered the doors situated under a pediment complete with dentil work I had all the common childhood thoughts such as "You could never do that anymore than you could fly to the moon," and "The year 2000 is so far away it will never come." However, one reserved childhood thought erupted and stayed with me for too many years—my imagination said I should say something only if I had something important to say which meant the idea was worth the listening. The idea was that the idea being related was more important than who said the idea. My voice relegated to the shadows of hearing so that others would not focus on my personality or ego. I didn't know to suspect that my voice had difficulty in recognizing and articulating a talent for introspection, but no experience to use the talent.

As I examined the books on the Lakewood Branch shelves I felt alive inside as if I had exercised my body. I was not learning to read great books, but learning to read. I felt I could be myself in the library. In the calm energies of the building I discovered some books were underlined many times, others with pencil marks in the margin, some hardly touched, some checked out many times by the same person and many, from the check-out record, never taken home.

I read to liberate myself from others. The library became a place to put things together, to take new steps, and to sense "people of words" around me. Even the dictionary provided insight. The books created a world of images that surfaced as day-dreaming which was considered child's play. But as my child's play formed in disorder and matured, I added language and organization to the visual images. My eyes saw the finer details. I selected the events and an order developed so that I could trust the visual images and eventually perform the function of creativity.

My real creative life began in my mid-thirties when I was at an age seeking a creative outlet to fill a void of unknown origins. I was aware that sometimes I had to fail to succeed, but I was willing to make the journey for the act of creation. My reading interests easily transferred to the art of seeing. An indescribable force within me wanted to say something that couldn't be said verbally. I couldn't exist passively and be standardized with whatever "the polls" said I needed. I rejected the traditional creative outlets for women such as needlepoint and flower arranging. With Joe Hedrick's photography expertise, I finally discovered my direction with an interest in photography. Don gave me a fine camera. I was at an age when time had taught me the rhythms of life and the beat was fast. I bypassed all the mediocre seminars, magazines and inferior equipment to concentrate on the best. As a homemaker, my normal occupations were counter to a creative life. I embarked on the art of seeing what the camera saw, unbeknownst to me, as another way to write and communicate. My learning was nothing but a greater aptitude than patience.

The time consuming craft of learning to see through the camera's eye, which sees more than I could possibly see, taught me sight was a function. To "look" uses a simple power of vision because only a single event was involved, requiring only a casual glance as a spectator. To "see" is a more complicated power of vision using perception, intuition, observation, imagination, anticipation and expression. To "see" is to look and understand as if a participant. The mature seer "sees" what he has learned to see. In a curious way I saw and collected knowledge to distribute in a creative effort.

Individuals who see the human spirit move subtly enjoy the availability of creativity which brings into existence something that has its own identity. Creativity comes to an individual with a first thought in a flash of nervous excitement in the brain representing the imagination and lasts only a few seconds. The imagined thought serves to breed another idea and the imagined thoughts fuse into a stable union. Einstein said that imagination was more important than knowledge. The creative thoughts and ideas with action translate into the reality of an art form such as a painting, sculpture, photograph or the written word.

I furthered my creative expression when I put my photographer's eye knowledge into a photography handbook. I organized a few rules and guidelines that I refreshed with my interpretations. I emphasized that most people think of themselves as ordinary, but ordinary was a person with a distinct level of energy and inward power. When one released that illusive, tiny part of his energized self, he was intimate for a fraction of a second with the camera and became extraordinary. That moment was when the complex components of the individual's energy, personality, physical presence, real or imagined history, and inner intensity collided and compressed into a presentation of an individual fully in control of his life. As the subject's energy combined with the lighting and contacted the photographic medium, a mystifying event happened to create an illusion that was not fully understandable, but accepted. As I acquired the skills and wrote about them, I was able to bring forth this energized self.

The christening of a child brings a family together even in distant cities such as Corpus Christi, Texas. Mark and his family fly to the seashore site of Donna's family. When the plane starts flying, Read asks, "Are we little now?" When the plane hits the runway to land, he says, "Are we driving now?"

I dress Carolyn in the christening dress that Mark and Donna had been christened in with their initials embroidered in the hem. With her godparents present at the Church of the Good Shepherd, Carolyn looks like a little puff of white clouds. Afterwards, there is a luncheon featuring pink and white cloths and flowers in the backyard. It is very fitting for a bright eyed, brown eyed baby.

When I return to my home, I take Read to the mall where a traveling petting zoo is installed. He almost gets out of the car, but decides the camel might get him. From the car he looks a long time at all the animals. Then he comments, "The baby elephant sure is big to be a baby."

On a wintery day, eight and one half months after his birth, Thomas is christened in the same white suit as his father and brother. After the minister of the First United Methodist Church in Lufkin christens him Jane puts him up on her shoulder so all can see this fine boy. Thomas looks around, gives one of his big smiles and utters a big sigh—oh, his timing is perfect.

The sandwich generation sprang into action with the news that my parents had bought a house next door to us with only twenty-six acres in between and a telephone call broke the news that Thomas needed surgery. Again, the unexpected happened. We wanted to make sense of what happened. I wanted to share some of the burden by carrying some of the pain for Thomas, Jane and Mark—a triple hurt. I was called to accompany Jane, Mark and Thomas to the large Houston hospital. On the one hundred twenty mile drive to the hospital, we stopped for a few minutes at a café. I held Thomas and Jane handed me a baby bottle of apple juice for him. As I reached for the bottle, so did Thomas. I knew then he would be all right. This was reality, not a dream. After the surgery when the nurses rolled Thomas into his room, Her Royal Majesty's Royal Scot Guards were playing in the parking lot for all the hospitalized children. What a good omen for Thomas. This episode was only one part of his life experience. His gift to us was he taught us by observing everything and something we never knew before. He accepted what was offered, acknowledged the enduring verities and that life was good.

Resiliently, with Halloween around the corner, Thomas wanted to be the "Cookie Monster" and Read wanted to be "Mickey Mouse."

Wednesday, January 1, 1986, Lufkin, Texas—A new year began sunny and bright. It's always good to start a new year with new goals, continuous ones. A list reaffirms the confusion and ups and downs of my life into a tidy vertical column. The list is fun, quick, condensed and helps me remember and contains a sense of accomplishment at year's end. The list reflects my instinct for order and a way to sum up what I expect for 1986. I am very blessed and I do have a grateful heart. Mother and Archie came down and brought ham and black eyed peas for good luck. I am so happy to have my mother and Archie here. I feel safe knowing they are here so I can help them. Sometimes in my writing a journal, the title of a book could be *Continued. . .* because all the good days and bad days of my life can't be completed on one page of my journal. Two major events in one day meant one page was not enough.

December 31, 1986, Dallas, Texas—1986 was a year full of events such as the explosion of the space ship Challenger. So tragic. Personally, the time goes by so fast I almost think there are two Christmases a year! So many in my family called me for emotional support and fortunately I was able to give to all.

6

A Level Site

Don and I exhaust looking at all other sites for our cabin and we are sure we select the right spot. In the spring we mark off the building site with our contractor, Brent Chapman. He gives us pointers, encourages us to level off a site on the mountainside, and our first assignment is to dig a water well.

At ninety feet we find good drinking water. The well is capped off with a pump and we are on our way to building our cabin.

Preparation for the day involves a moisturizer, barrier cream, and eye emollient, all under a foundation make-up to enhance not dominate.

I wear my Monte Cristo hat which has retained its shape with only three turquoise pins. I am hoping I am not classified as an old timer for wearing a hat. Besides, in the mountains, I don't wear a hat to get a better seat in a fine restaurant.

My shirt is a solid navy blue, not a blue iris hue, long sleeve shirt cut like a man's dress shirt with a button down collar and a button on the cuff. My blue substitutes for black because although black is sleek and chic, it doesn't fit the attitude of my inner spirit and character. It is easy to roll my sleeve up to mid-arm to make three-quarter-length sleeves.

I am dressed for the day in my dark blue, blue jeans with copper rivets to reinforce pocket corners. They do not come from a jeans boutique.

Peeking out of my back blue jeans pocket is a royal blue handkerchief with a wide white border stripe intersecting at each corner to give it vibrancy. If I have a red one, it is more noteworthy because it will not show lipstick blotting. Regardless of the color my handkerchief has become an indispensable part of my wardrobe even though Kleenex has come of age. Before tattoos, piercings, pink hair, facial glitter, my handkerchief expresses my uniqueness and individuality. My collection of handkerchiefs is kept in a peach colored satin-lined folder, a color once considered risqué.

My shoes for the day are low top, lightweight tennis shoes for the extra cushioning, but no see-through soles or blinking red lights. Round metal grommets hold the laces in place. I do not choose white tennis shoes that stay indoors, but the not-so-popular navy blue for outdoors with little integrated design.

My watch with its navy leather band and quartz battery doesn't need winding. In the dark it illuminates the hour, minute and second hands. The timepiece shows me that the future has arrived much quicker than I think. It is now. Although time doesn't dominate I don't want to allow the "now" to only be a prelude to the "next." I want to be alive in the present moment—not unbroken, but finishing this, so I can get to something else. Who can guess that one day an iPhone or iPad will almost replace a watch?

With a building permit in order, a small bulldozer driven by Mr. John Graeser, claims a trail up the side of the mountain to our building site. One hundred twenty-five year old trees are leveled which gives us an eerie feeling. The trunks are stripped of their limbs and dragged to a pile near the road. The pile will be burned after the first snow.

This dirt work is the beginning of our driveway to the cabin. It will be covered with gravel for easy access.

Then a huge Komatsu bulldozer, too heavy for our river bridge, fords the river just past where the creek and river meet, to reach our building site. Huge amounts of dirt and boulders are removed from the mountain. Rocks fall down the mountain. We have to cut into the mountain side enough to allow ten feet behind the house which will accommodate the blade of the snow removal equipment. The grade of the lot does not need to slope. But the land needs to pitch away from the house. The bulldozer carves from the original dirt formation an area 58 x 26 feet and three feet deep. The outside edge of the opening provides the foundation for the log walls. The inside dimensions provide the crawl space under the house because there is no basement.

I ride in the bulldozer when Mr. Graeser agrees to move several flat boulders to the building site. He lifts the rocks like lifting an egg and places several large, flat rocks at the far edge of the future yard. Here I envision sitting to view the surroundings. A level site soon appears large enough to accommodate the house, driveway and a parking area which will be out of direct sight from the living room window. The view will include Lady Fingers and the mountain we see on the way to South Fork. We mark off the lot and set the view. That night after the site preparation Don dreams of building the house all night and I dream that I manually push the bulldozer up the hill.

Discussions on a house plan start and revolve around Mother's cabin floor plan, and the ideas start flowing. The cabin floor plan has to fit into a long narrow expanse accommodating the house, privacy, driveway and grassy yard for our grandchildren's play. Then a trench is dug uphill from the well near the road to the house site to house the water line with a shelf for the telephone and electric lines. We don't want any utility lines to show and block our views.

Don erects a homemade sign at the base of the driveway, "Formal Opening, Fall, 1987."

7

Plans for the Foundation

Now the process begins of transferring my ideas to paper for Brent to implement. I know the basic length and width dimensions, the basic layout of rooms to fit our needs, and most importantly the views. Using my mother's basic floor plan for her cabin I draw rough, freehand sketches of our floor plan with all the main rooms on one floor to accommodate us in our old age. For old age is just a few years past my actual age. This sketch records my ideas for later use. It is a way to try out different ideas, establish a custom feel, and settle on the composition before undertaking a finished plan. My sketch is a diagram, like metaphors, as a means of design collaboration with the draft person, Linda Langston, who does the technical drawing.

With Linda's discipline of creating standardized technical drawings used by architects, interior designers, design engineers and related professionals, the floor plan begins to shape on paper using line thickness, text size, symbols, dimensioning and notations—all ideally interpreted in only one way. She gives me graphic communications that transform ideas into a physical form.

With precision, Linda incorporates the sketch into parallel lines forming the outside dimensions of 58 x 26 feet. With no intended angles less than ninety degrees, arcs or circles, a T-square becomes the main drawing tool. Templates are used for recurring objects. All are done with accuracy and attention to detail in the two-dimensional drawing.

This house will not be "motherless" or "fatherless." Don and I will accept responsibility for its building and for any plan changes.

With the view of Lady Fingers to the west the most important element, the living room, is placed on the west side. The dining room is part of the living room. The galley shaped kitchen faces north to the road with a window to see the comings and goings of our neighbors. A stairway backs the living room fireplace. The utility room is tucked underneath the stairway. Two bedrooms form the east side. The master bedroom dressing area and bath are on the road side with views to the big lake; the guest bedroom with a private bath faces the driveway with a view of the mountainside sloping upwards to the Rio Grande National Forest boundary.

It is not easy to throw away or even give away any books so we add a shelf for noteworthy books in the area before one enters the stairway. Upstairs are the game room, two bedrooms and one large bathroom. Each bedroom has a distinct view of Lady Fingers and the big lake.

From my primary home, with the house plan complete, we send the drawings to Brent for a bid. He makes sure the parts fit together. The front porch is modified to not interfere with the front window, and the dormer window upstairs is modified to allow for logs to show underneath.

While waiting for the Brent's reply, I spend time with my grandchildren.

At our primary home when Read stays with us, I put him in my bed, lie down beside him and tell him a story. I want to give part of myself to Read and I find that I get back more than I give. I tell Read about a little boy named "Read." "Once upon a time there was a little boy named Read. He went to the zoo and saw lots of animals and lots of birds—a blue bird, then a sparrow, a robin red breast, a hummingbird and a mockingbird." Before I continue with the story, Read interjects: "Don't forget naked as a jay bird." The moment is silent laughter to not deter his childlike thinking which one day will be fine inductive reasoning. When he turns on his right side, I know he is going to sleep.

At home, Read is asked what does he do at church school and he replies, "I teach."

At Easter time, Read wants to buy some Easter eggs and sit on them to hatch them out.

Read as a three year old, begins to put up things at our house that might hurt Thomas—a letter opener, any medicine.

Don and I take five year old Read to the Crown Colony Country Club for dinner. He is proud of his navy blazer and penny loafers. He orders steak, baked potato, French fries and pastry from the pastry cart. He talks of the decorative radish and watercress on his plate. He knows about parsley. After dinner he takes a bite of radish and says, "It tastes like apple." When he picks up the watercress he asks me, "Is there a special way to hold it?" Don says, "It tastes like weeds." Read chews and says, "It does taste like grass."

Thomas now stands in bed and crawls and when his mother talks of the sky, he looks up, shakes his head when she says, "no-no" and makes a noise when she says "elephant." He is beginning to walk and with his finger dexterity holds on to your hand. I start walking with him right where he is. He walks with his left hand up holding onto my right finger. So when he walks by himself he holds his left hand up out of habit.

Thomas gives us a completely new perspective to see the world. With his warm brown eyes and refined look he charms us by saying, "This is a wonderful day." Later he tells us that one of his grandmothers knows about the Bible, the other grandmother knows about manners. We take nothing for granted.

Later Thomas has me tell him a story. Then he asks, "What is a story?" We talk of the elements of a story such as it's telling of something happening, that it is true or imagined, is written or told, and it's shorter than a novel. I ask Thomas to tell me a story. He hesitates and finally tells a short story, then another short story and another. Soon he tells me a long story. At nighttime just as he goes to sleep he starts a story and when he awakes in the morning, he immediately continues his story.

Carolyn crawls out her primary home front door that has blown open. She is on her way down the sidewalk. When Donna calls to her to come back, Carolyn looks back and with a look that says, "Don't bother me, I'm on my way to town."

I am staying in Carolyn's primary home bedroom and still asleep in the early, early morning. Carolyn stands up in her bed and says "Hi." I ignore her and after she says "Hi" ten times. I say "Hi." She is ready for the day. I know then that she will be a "people person." She will comfort herself with elegance in a measured tone in all that she does and speak.

When Brent presents the bid on building the cabin, it is more than we want or have to spend on the house. We work on cutting out a lot of fluff and I learn again the meaning of change to allow things to move along. We sign the final papers. Then walk the site among tall, vertical trees to confirm a panoramic view that is horizontal and wide.

Staying at Mother's cabin while our cabin is under construction, I begin traveling from my primary home in Lufkin to Mother's cabin to supervise the building. Just before I leave Mother's cabin, I review what Brent will be doing for the next two to three weeks when I return from Lufkin.

Another dimension is added to my life when my third grandson is born, John Mark Reily. About mid-morning Mark comes out of the delivery room beaming with the news that his third son is born with hazel colored eyes. At birth he has a distinct, commanding look, and I can see both Thomas and Read in his face. John Mark commands with a youthful, calming strength on the side of handsome.

Everyone helps him see the connections between generations with his name, John Mark. Jane and Mark use a traditional name for his first and second name. Plus his second name honors his father. He is tied to his roots and belongs to a family and community along with an attic full of treasures. We have seen changes in our lifetime with more focus on "being there" for him. We respect him and when he first responds, we talk in sentences to him, not "baby talk." We default to simplicity because there is no lack of respect from him. We reciprocate with respect for him. We will always be there for him as we make meaningful memories. Yet, we know his starting from the bottom produces knowledge which is his protection.

A 1 3/4 x 1 3/4 inch pin with seven points of turquoise and silver within a circular design is added to my Monte Cristo hat.

John Mark is christened in the First United Methodist Church in Lufkin wearing the same white suit as his brothers. Thomas and Read join his parents with John at the altar. John is all smiles and looks at the congregation when his head is sprinkled. He enjoys the occasion and somehow knows it is his day.

All the family joins in teaching John Mark his natural manners by setting a good example.

John can handle all the love you can give him. He puts no obstacles in our way to let us love him. He minds well and gives the best hugs as if they are medicine.

I am grandmother for fourth time and now a much gentler grandmother. Regardless of how many times, it is still a gift, a present. John Mark, soon to be called John, will teach us to work as a team so he will not drop out of our awareness.

It's easy to learn John's favorite color is green which matches my favorite color. This sharing of favorite colors strengthens our relationship because we present him everything in green.

That year just as Christmas ends a "Pete and Repeat" doll is opened. John Mark and Read settle in for the night. John has a hard time going to sleep and is crying. Every time he cries, the Pete and Repeat doll cries. It's a good laugh for the parents.

I do not hesitate to play with my grandchildren on the grass or carpet. I even retrieve them in the McDonald's pit of colored balls with a "high five." Our play brings us together with a pause from the world.

Jane and Mark kill a mouse at their house and Read keeps talking about it. Finally, Jane says, "Read, stop thinking about the mouse, change your thinking." Read asks, "How do you change your thinking?" He begins the ability to think, to stretch his mind beyond the obvious. Although thinking is hard work, step by step, he will apply his knowledge to new situations then look at all avenues and patterns.

Thursday, January 1, 1987, Dallas, Texas—Would you believe that when I wrote the last word for December 31, 1986, I ran out of ink? So I'm beginning 1987 with the freshest of ink. Once again I've considered my goals for the year. I met a lot of my goals I set last year and hope to do the same this year. It's a good challenge and I feel quite rewarded. 1987 looks good to me and my family. I am very blessed. Don and I spent the day watching TV bowl games. As Dear Abby says, "Any man watching more than nine hours of football games on TV can be declared legally dead." I have waited a long time to have my Dallas apartment and it is so pleasurable.

Thursday, December 31, 1987, South Fork, Colorado— At the cabin we have no draperies, so we could see the clear, nearly full moon out the bedroom window last night. 1987 has been the year of building the log cabin. I made seven or eight round trips to direct the building. It was literally a creation from choosing the building site to today. I do enjoy building as a way of creating with hundreds of details. As I read over my goals for 1987, I found I accomplished a great deal of them eager to continue those I didn't finish and content to have some goals that are always ongoing. I have been blessed with family and friends. I look forward to '88 which has a good rhythmic sound.

Don and I were fully into the sandwich generation with Mother, Archie and my mother-in-law Julia Belle Holley Reily, our children with their spouses, and our grandchildren. With each we tried to honor their dignity and self-esteem, establish a line between independence and safety, and help them substitute individuality for independence. It was like being caught between a tiny evergreen tree fighting for space, an old giant redwood tree, and a smaller oak tree with limbs spreading every way. There were rigid boundaries that I didn't step across, but I didn't know it was a line until I stepped over it.

Nobody told me how to be a parent to my parents. I gave each choices and self-dignity.

I was not an only child, but I gave of my time ungrudgingly. To be any other way to my parents and mother-in-law would be uncomfortable. I was gracious as well as kind and kept harmony with Robert and Morten.

It began with helping my parents with their mail, shopping, paying bills and then managing their entire lives. For them everyday tasks became monumental. I plugged into the senior network. I recognized that at this time in my life, this was what I was doing.

Mother said there was no "going of the mind" in our family. Was she reassuring me or her? I was mothering Mother, she only mothered the past.

I questioned whether I would spend more time caring for parents than children? Were the mommy years less difficult than the parent-care years? Caregiving wasn't easy, but it was essential to rescue them when needed, deflect any anger with humor and don't demean them for just being old. There was little need to fault my parents for the aging process.

I reciprocated Mother for being a good parent and for her sacrifices by being a good parent to my children and now to her. I just redesigned my life. When I was little and needed something, Mother was there. She had an uncanny ability to place her children in the right place at the right time of their lives. Now when she needed something, I was there day to day.

Mother was not demanding and did not believe life was linear and her old age was a straight line to the end. She was just more of what she was in her youth—a good attitude. I was compassionately firm in keeping her safe to live longer. I coped with my feelings by acknowledging that Mother won't get better. As I spent time with her, I learned of her as a person with so much wisdom. There were moments of humor, warmth and love, so I welcomed them. She was quite optimistic about the future.

In my mind's eye, my mother was still in her prime. Her face had wrinkles, character lines but not old because of energy, enthusiasm and excitement about living—this separated the aging from the old. There was a purpose to get up every day. But she was among the old, old and these were her remaining years. I knew that family took care of family, although soon it would be the old taking care of the older.

I gifted my mother by my taking care of myself, so I could take care of her. If I didn't set aside my time, and if I did too much I would be angry, so I took care of myself. I didn't lose sight of my own life as I began to balance role reversal.

I traced the action part of my writing life from one simple act. I read the line attributed to Robert Louis Stevenson, "A friend is a gift from you to yourself." Often I felt the quote and thought the quote was an insightful thought to remember. So, unbeknownst to me, I began my writing life by typing the quotation on notebook paper. I inserted the page into a black 7 x 9 inch notebook with a label on the front for my name. The notebook filled quickly with additional thoughts spilling over to yellow legal pads.

The volume of typed and handwritten words finally overwhelmed me. I didn't know what to do with the notes, yet I couldn't discard them. By 1970 I had become a book buyer. I had read, categorized and placed my favorite books in the bookends on my bedside table. *The Lord Is My Shepherd* by Roy L. Smith stood at the beginning of my bookends. Smith wrote of the "Twenty-third Psalm" not as a song but as an assertion of faith in God that nothing one needs will be lacking. Smith published with no publication date because the message was timeless. *Men to Match My Mountains* by Irving Stone stood tall in the bookends. Stone wrote of a colorful gallery of characters who tamed the West and the West tamed them. These people were larger than life and matched the mountains and shaped American history. My love for Stone's book periodically insisted I reread it. The bookends concluded with *Gift from the Sea*, published in 1955 by Anne Morrow Lindbergh.

Lindbergh not afraid to spend time, free of the clutter of constant music, talk and companionship spent a week alone in her own space at the beach. Here she wrote eight meditative essays telling of her life's experiences as she discovered the seashore had gifts to give. Lindbergh wrote of the pattern of the tides and the life of the seashells that revealed a pattern of the values of an inner life. Lindbergh, probably, with a teacup in hand and to feed her nurturing soul said, "I need to sit down and pause for a moment with a mind free of yesterday's schedule to free my mind to receive the gifts from the sea."

Eight years after Lindbergh's book, Betty Friedan wrote her landmark 1963 book, *The Feminine Mystique*. Friedan described the clash between the education women were receiving and how they were expected to live the remainder of their lives.

At my bedside was not only a collection of books but a collection of knowledge. Out of my imagination erupted a flash of nervous excitement. A simple solution for my notes was to write a book combining my three favorite books. What better place to learn to write than from the "best." Because I was not educated as a writer, I embarked on a journey of unaided discovery rather than one of instruction.

Webster defined a writer as one who wrote as an occupation. If that was the proper definition, then with my level of writing, when did I call myself a writer?

My definition of a writer was one who wrote and told a story. Yet, at parties I did not want to be introduced, "She's trying to write a book." Maybe I was an apprentice-writer.

When I told my friends and family I was writing a book, most responded with silence, some with a hum, some with "don't talk about it because I will destroy it" and one gave me a fine typewriter.

As most women writers, I began writing of what I knew best. Novice writers learned to write from their enthusiasm of what they read and knew. I used my beloved mountains as the background for my voice that was clear from the inside but didn't instantly follow my creative needs.

I wrote in longhand with a fountain pen of a long gone era which allowed me to write anywhere and to slow down the thinking process. I glided the writing instrument against the paper for resistance. The line of words was controlled by my hand. The feeling of touching the paper led me to the music of language arranged in my particular rhythmic manner. I blotted the ink slowly on the lined page because often I wrote before I was ready. I did not wait to be inspired to write, but I wrote to find inspiration. I found freedom in the margins and between the lines as I was learning to write by writing. There was no word processor's blinking cursor urging me to hurry. I wrote hoping to place the spoken language onto a written page because that's another way people communicated. I wanted to reach out with language one heard and saw simultaneously. The satisfaction was seeing the words form and knowing writing was reducing to the essentials. I was always glad for what I omitted. There was no writer's block, only decisions as to what to do next. If I knew what would happen next I probably wouldn't write.

Writing involved a level of privacy and I needed isolation. I accomplished more when alone. Yet, I didn't have a room with a sign taped to the closed door, "Private, No Entry Without Personal Invitation."

Once I started writing the room wasn't as important as finding my own private space where the writing allowed me to understand what I had already learned and told me how I arrived here. I redefined myself with the material surrounding me as I brought out the depth of my heart. The room adhered to my five senses because I saw how the sunlight oozed in carefully. I heard the noise only from the outside world as I wrote to the pursuit of silence. I touched the paper to add to the tactile environment. There was only a cup of tea by my desk to invigorate my taste buds. And I noted there was no potpourri to violate the room. I compounded my writing daily and I tried to stop for the day at a high point so the next day I would know where to begin.

Just as important as the room, a much needed level of social engagement was the gathering of field information and the collecting of research. I recognized a talent for surrounding myself with talented people.

I wrote as a freelance writer bringing assets of freedom, independence, and a greater variety of interests. I added the liabilities of insecurity and rejection, rode on an emotional roller coaster, and was aware of my own faults. All these assets and liabilities counterbalanced the understanding that knowledge without my effort was worse than not having knowledge.

The continuous journey for which I was solely responsible

was not approached with any particular method but merely hard work in the right direction.

All my notes were then emancipated from the notebooks and tablets by scissoring each and "cutting and scotch taping" them into a pile of ten chapters with thirty-three essays. This was my best effort at a book proposal or outline giving the book a broad structure and direction for my self-disclosing in print.

Encouragement came when Mary Twohig Wilson of Angelina College had me read aloud a chapter. It was all I could do to keep my voice from cracking. It filled my heart when I read aloud what I've read so many times silently. Mary told me that I could do one of three things: burn the book as if I had no talent; photocopy a copy for my family and friends; or publish the book. The praise fueled my passion and I understood Einstein's remark, "the personal corruption of praise."

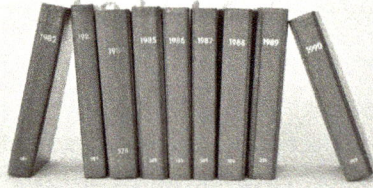

8

The Logs Form a Cabin

I arrive at my writing headquarters at my mother's cabin. Our cabin, a creative effort, begins forming with my supervision and a measuring tape precise to 1/16 of an inch.

I always remove the night time cleansing cream using my facial CleanSoft. Using the light to heaviest cream I apply a moisturizer, barrier cream, an advanced moisturizer, then a high energy repair wear cream and eye emollient. I want to contour the wrinkles around my eyes with enough lines to display an emotion and respect the wrinkles. All the creams disappear as I rub them into my skin. The tinted foundation make-up blends with my skin tone, conceals imperfections, and gives a smooth look. With the application of makeup as an art, I add a subtle eye make-up cream shadow over my eyelids and beneath my brows with an easy finger application so that it won't streak, move around or even crease.

Intermittently I wear my Monte Cristo hat with four silver and turquoise pins. Wearing this hat is a prelude to getting use to something on your head before everyone wears baseball hats.

Again, I put on a solid color, blue turquoise cotton T-shirt which has a collar and no logo on the left breast. There are no wise or racy savings waiting to be read and demanding that you relate to the message. If I do wear a T-shirt with a saying, it will only divert your attention from the traumas of the world for a few moments.

I dress for comfort in my slacks that are a pull-on pant with a tunnel elastic waistband that holds a nylon web belt and buckle. The fabric is lightweight and soft with quick drying properties. There is a left side cargo pocket with a hanging bag and zipper closure.

My on-seam side pockets hold a handkerchief that I not only need, but enjoy for how it makes me feel and what it helps me remember. For years four small square pieces of fabric had resided in a small, slim box in my attic with a note attached saying it is from my grandmother. After years I remove them from the box, wash them to turn them white, but they stay ecru colored from age. In one corner someone had embroidered different designs in greens, peaches, yellow, gold and purple.

My walking involves only walking to and from our cabin to mother's cabin which is unintentional exercise, like doing chores. My shoes enable me to navigate walking on real ground like grass, dirt, fallen leaves, and sand. My absorbent socks allow my feet to breathe.

I don't allow my watch and the pace of our lives to create a chasm between my emotions and thoughts which function at different speeds. I process my thoughts faster than my emotions, but I'm allowing myself to slow down to relax and slow down the rhythm so I can experience the exhilaration. The important event is taking place and I am enjoying the moment, not longing for the end result. I never recover lost time, but who cares.

Seeing the first stages of building the cabin, my excitement is justified because the three rows of concrete blocks, which had to be right, with a layer of Styrofoam on the inside form the foundation for the logs on the bulldozer-carved dirt wall. On the outside the two bottom rows of concrete blocks are painted with black tar to protect them from the snow accumulation. These concrete blocks support a series of floor joists to distribute the weight. A 2 x 6 inch board on top of the row of blocks forms the remainder of the foundation and is followed by plywood sub-flooring. When Don sees the foundation, he turns to me and gives me a hug.

The first row of rasped-down-to-smooth logs are placed on the sub-flooring. Large ten inch nails are driven into each first row of logs to secure them to the foundation. In the utility room a hole is cut for access to the underbelly/crawl space with lights underneath. Four vents for ventilation are placed, one of each side of the house. The house forms as each row of logs is added with ten inch nails on top of the previous row of logs. With five rows of logs, the spaces for the double pane windows are set. I will see through some of them that morning has broken, and through some the exiting of the day.

Double-pane, custom Marvin windows are ordered. The Ponderosa Pine windows, with sash casings, insulate our cabin. Weather stripping cuts energy costs and provides negative leaks for wind, water and air filtration. The pine accepts stain or varnish. With no arches and single glide partitions, beauty and safety is pronounced. They can be opened and closed and some remain closed.

Eleven rows of logs are laid with headers on top for the large picture window openings which provide a rectangular landscape. The second floor is formed with floor joists and a sub-flooring of plywood. Then a stairwell of twelve steps with vertical eight inch risers and horizontal eleven inch treads is installed. A stairway handrail on the left of the stairs will help me and my wobbly friends. Each step brings steps of the mind such as distractions, music, strength and even hope. The thirteenth step ends on the second floor. When I reach the top stair on a clear day I can see the sunrise and sunset glow through the game room window. The bottom step will lead to a small table housing a note pad and pencil for future scribbling on 4 x 6 inch note paper. It's assumed the notes are to be kind to others, be helpful, considerate, and compassionate as humanly as possible.

Twenty logs form each wall. The one dormer window is changed to allow the logs to show in front of the house. I mix the Sikkens stain of three parts natural oak and one part antique gray. The pigment coating colors the wood. With three coats, the Sikkens stain finishes, preserves and protects the logs.

The roof rafters are added. A plywood decking and an autumn brown Desert Tan shingle roof "dry in" the house. The house measures twenty-six feet from ground to the peak of the roof. An opening is left for the brick chimney and flashing. One ceiling door is cut to provide access to the attic. Insulation installed in the attic will ward off some cold weather. The soffit, fascia and eaves are roughed in. Brown gutters and down spouts are added.

As an after-thought, or initial mistake, electrical heat tapes on the roof are installed to dispose of the snow and ice accumulation. The heat tape is put in a zigzag pattern so the upper loops extend on the shingle into an area over the heated portion of the house. The bottom loops extend beyond the roof overhang and into the gutter and down spouts.

Twelve inch sonar tubes filled with concrete make the concrete support posts for the deck. A large wooden deck surrounds the house on the living room and dining room side. The deck is an outdoor room with a front-row seat to the view, a place to sit and unwind, and dine. Three feet wide deck walkways extend on two sides. The railings are vertical and close together so a small child's head will not fit through the slats. Three gates with latches are built to enclose the entire deck.

A grouping of wooden chairs, sofa, low table and dining table makes it possible for us to have a sense of being far away. The deck becomes a repository for our memories.

Accessories for the deck include four feet wide steps in the front, side and back, outside faucets, porch lights, outside flood lights, and three doorbells for the three doors.

Next to the front gate and brick walkway is a flagpole to raise the United States flag. Its unfurled stars and stripes is our quest for a just society for all Americans. Hopefully, Americans are bound together with the flag as a symbol of shared hope and mutual respect. The flag when hoisted briskly is a daily symbol that our family is "in residence." It never touches the ground and gains our respect.

Although we are Texas bred, underneath the United States flag we hoist the Colorado state flag with its three alternate stripes of equal width, the two outer stripes of the same blue as our national flag. Within the stripes is a circular red "C," the same red in the national flag. Inside the "C" is a golden disk.

When we leave the cabin, we lower the flags ceremoniously and fold the United States flag into twelve folds. Although not officially recognized, the folds mean life, eternal life, in honor of all veterans, our need of divine guidance, our love for our country, as a tribute to Armed Forces, honor of mothers, all women, fathers and finally the God of the Old Testament.

9

The Interior Makes the Cabin

On the inside of the layer of logs is a thin layer of felt, a 1 1/2 inch Styrofoam layer, a 4 mil plastic sheet, followed by 1/8 inch sheetrock. The final layer is 1/4 inch tongue and grove spruce or aspen paneling or vinyl covered sheet rock. Ready-made door openings are installed in the framing. The framing allows for the electrical, ceiling fans, and circuit breaker.

Acoustical batting, in some inside walls, deadens the sound. The brown and glass outside doors are hung and the storm doors with high and low glass and screen are hung according to the wind that blows hard through the valley.

The partitions begin forming and make rooms so we can envision the house and begin walking through.

I ready myself. I now avoid the direct sun and add a face cream with sun screen as a barrier to protect from the sun and look as young as possible. I know that sooner or later, with age my face shortens, chin moves back, cheeks hollow, nose and ears enlarge, and more wrinkles appear. With the cosmetic creams I add a dark spot corrector and anti-aging products. I do not finalize my foundation make-up with a face powder. I want a "dewy" look, not a "dry skin" look.

I place my Monte Cristo hat with four turquoise and silver pins on my head in a jaunty angle because the creation of the cabin is coming to fruition. I have reason to brag.

My shirt choice of a plaid, man-made polyester with cotton is not an afterthought, but varies with the neutral colored khaki slacks. The cloth has interlocking stripes in multiple cool colors. I am not consistently confounded by color and perplexedly by pattern. Bright colors absorb the heat more and are more noticeable so that every time I wear it, people say, "Oh, I always like that shirt."

The day is scheduled for me to wear my twill, khaki slacks that feel substantial but wash to softness. The straight leg fit is double-pleated with no cuffs, no flap on the back pocket, and no extra belt loops which make them beyond the commonplace. These slacks will be remembered by all women as they notice the fashion details.

The large, light tan, embroidered monogram "N" on my white handkerchief brings a feeling of dignity and recognition. The intention is to make non-verbal communication.

In defense of women's fashion, my shoes are rather mannish as women's fashion often become more and more like men. The navy walking shoes with laces are not too soft, have cushioned insoles and easily hold my arch supports. Not unlike children, I always double knot the shoelaces.

With the new digital watches, I choose to rely on my timepiece showing the hour, minute, second, day and date. Doing so gives me a different attitude than the current popular digital watch. Although the means of telling time has changed, the daily rhythms of my life within the human community have not changed. Regardless of the timepiece, procrastination steals from time and life demands punctuality. But if everyone is late, then everyone is on time.

The first walk through the halls delivers us into large, open spaces. As we walk through the halls the patterns of light shift their slanted design as the light comes through the picture windows and doors. Without the light there is no life because light makes things visible and brings humanity to take me beyond time and its limitations.

Then with a further walk through we decide to make the master bedroom one large room rather than two small ones. We start with a blank space and add touches for our retreat and interests such as a writing desk, reading area, and television. All these interests indicate we are making a commitment to relax. We provide for chairs with ottomans, pillows, good lighting, and a side table. We add telephone jacks, television cables, smoke alarms and baseboard heaters throughout the house. Inside our master dressing room are two chests of drawers. They begin as empty, not like the drawers of my mind filled with experiences from childhood to the present. The drawers, wide and narrow when open and full, will reveal not only the contents but the light and dark of life to declare our past.

Recessed lighting fixtures in the sheet rock ceilings provide additional light. Pocket doors aid where space is limited. All the doors have polished brass door knobs.

Plumbing is installed beneath the house with a water filter and the pipes slant downhill to facilitate draining to winterize the house.

A huge hole in the front yard for the 1,250 gallon septic tank is covered with top soil from the dredges of the ponds in the valley.

The vinyl covered sheetrock is installed. Paneled rooms have applied Sikken stains of one part dark oak and five parts colorless. The brick fireplace is built with a damper and a forty-two inch Heatilator with glass doors. The walls and each room with a thermostat will create an economy of heat and cold so that we experience various temperatures as we go from room to room.

The kitchen cabinets are installed with laminate because granite counters are not in vogue. Vinyl covers the kitchen floor. I select the same pattern of carpet: gray carpet for downstairs and tan carpet for upstairs with no pad or shoe molding.

The wall trim is painted tan upstairs and gray downstairs with matching base molding.

With left-over sheetrock, the four attic storage areas are patched over the framing. The area will hold fishing gear, yard tools, unused paint, carpet and vinyl, and my encyclopedias. One storage area is reserved for the grandchildren's playhouse complete with toys. In time I know these storage areas will fill and I will have to decide what is cluttering up the space and what is cluttering up my mental space and let go of what we treasure to make room for more. As we clean out the areas, the hard part is to know what to do with the items. As we clear the areas, I will have a clear vision of what I really have to work with and what we really need. When others talk of building a storage shed, I know more de-cluttering is needed. Hoarding is not in our vocabulary.

The entrance doors are brown with sliding glass windows at the top.

Don terraces the back driveway incline with seeds and matting. Then he covers the incline with vertical rows of small, tall, dead aspen trunks. He sows a mixture of grass seeds on the front and back yards.

At home we gather up some furnishings from the attic for the cabin. Don calls these rooms so furnished as our "furniture cemetery."

New beds are ordered and installed. Everyone will have a bed that they love and at the end of each day feels like a well-deserved reward, almost like a diploma, and like the pot of gold at the end of the rainbow with a chocolate truffle.

I select three trundle beds for my grandchildren and place them in the "Trundle Room." They save space, are simple and rugged to last for years, and the grandchildren can live on them, not around them. Any nicks only add to the character of the trundle.

In my decorating skills, I think a deer horn chandelier is appropriate over the dining table. I bring one that measures three feet in diameter, nineteen inches high with eight brass candelabra lights and try it over Mother's dining table. It looks good. So we place one over the dining table at our cabin. It claims the empty space and creates intricate shadows. All our men friends call it, "Nancy's horny chandelier." So I change it to my "antler chandelier."

Earlier, we saw a dining room table that seated eight with extensions to seat twelve. Don buys the dining room table and surprises me when it is delivered. It is not two saw horses supporting a plywood sheet, but rather patrician binding my family together. The formal living room is vanishing to the family room, but the dining area is here to stay. It is part of the family room, much like a glamorous visitor with centerpieces and table settings.

***

Not too absorbed in building I make time for my family. Donna, Carolyn and I visit the site. Carolyn makes a dash for the stairs. Since she has just celebrated her second birthday, she keeps saying "I'm two at the party." When we stay at Mother's house, we put out bread for the chip monks and Carolyn keeps picking up the bread crumbs to eat.

As Donna, Carolyn and I depart the site and drive home,

Carolyn gets restless in her car seat and keeps saying, "I'm stuck." Carolyn at her home wants to "swim suit" every day.

Thomas does not fare too well at his first day of nursery school. About 11:00 am the teacher calls Jane to come get Thomas because he can't quit crying. When Thomas gets home and becomes quiet, he says, "I cried all through school just like this, 'Boo Hoo.'" He even imitates the cry.

Later Mark calls me and says, "Mother, we need help getting to your mother's cabin." I agree to go with him, Jane and three grandsons. All of us load into one car for the three hour trip to Dallas where we spend the night and fly the next day to our cabin site. After one hour in the car we stop for a rest room break. Mark comments to me, "Mother, we are making thirty-five miles an hour." For our airplane flight I make lots of peanut butter sandwiches for the hour and a half trip. We sit in the front seats facing each other and the sandwiches entertain them for the entire trip.

While at Mother's cabin, John crawls in the hallway which makes a circle and looks my way when Jane says "Grandmother."

Read catches a fish and when Mark asks him whether he wants to eat it or throw it back in the water: Read says to eat it. Mark guts the fish and Read then declares he doesn't want to eat it and is upset at the results.

When Read is playing in the front yard, Thomas hears him and comes out the back door. Thomas asks me to show him how to get to the front yard.

John is just big enough to sit under the red back porch at mother's cabin and dig in the dirt.

Later at the cabin I take John to town. He says, "There's the river" and when the road leaves the river and returns to the river John says, "There's another river." There is only one river to cross.

Four year old John Mark makes us a Valentine. In his attempt to get everything right, when he hands it to me he asks, "Am I to leave it here or take it with me?"

One day Mother and I are talking about the movie star and celebrity, Elizabeth Taylor. John Mark hears us and asks, "Who is Elizabeth Taylor?" We explain to him that she is a famous movie star. He asks, "Is she as famous as Emmitt Smith?"

In late fall of 1987, I have a final walk through of our cabin. When we return the house will be complete. There is power in our return. We know we will open the door to our cabin to satisfy our comfort cravings, private lives, joys and sorrows as we renew strength for another day, whatever it brings. Then as we enter the front door, we know that our absence has a presence. We feel, smell and hear as we reach for the light switch that home is a place, a feeling, and a state of mind.

Our design takes several paths and we aren't sure which style we achieve. The glass picture windows allow participation with the sun, moon, rain and snow. With picture windows we are half inside and half outside, but we know we need picture window privacy.

We don't want heavy draperies that cover the entire wall when pulled open. We choose to cover the windows and door windows with custom made Roman shades that allow the full window to show. The length and width of each window is measured. A formula of the length of the window divided by five, plus length of window plus one inch; and the width measured with two inches on each side, determines the amount of fabric. Each room has its own personality and different fabric. Blackout lining controls the light, provides privacy, and gives a uniform appearance when seen from the outside. A 1 x 2 inch board is mounted at the top of each Roman shade and mounted to the wall. The fabric forms a cornice board.

A thin cord passes through plastic rings glued to the underside and anchors to a pulley system for raising the shades, like a Venetian blind, into perfect folds. A locking system for the pulley cord is attached to the side of the window for raising and lowering the shades. Only one small window is dressed with a pleated teardrop style. With such a small opening, it will be hard to fling any of the bad habits stressed in an instruction manual out the window, but they can be coaxed down the stairs to the main living area window where love flies in.

When I slowly open the Roman shades just a crack, it's like opening my eyelids slowly. The scene is not monotonous reading like the best of the Dick and Jane readers, but a revelation of my eyes blending the colors from the straight brown deck railing, wavering green spruce trees and the ever present blue sky. It's like the beginning of a rainbow. All the elements perform right before my eyes.

To open them abruptly is like the world exploding on me with all its lighting. I have to step back a few paces to leave my childhood spring landscape behind. It is as if I wake up and find myself in a place that already exists—a distinctive spring though almost half-past winter.

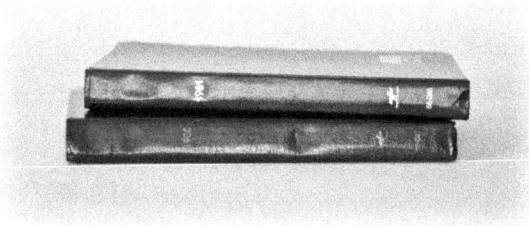

10

In Residence at the Cabin

By now my face requires cleansing cream, astringent to give a sensation of freshness, moisturizer, advanced moisturizer, repair wear cream and an anti-aging cream, and a skin tone enhancer with SPF20—all to fight the effects of time. An enriched cream covers my eyelids and under my brow. My eyelashes are enhanced with three coats of brown/black mascara. Lipstick still covers my lips and serves as rouge on my cheeks. I have gone the gamut—cover-up, emphasize, illuminate, minimize, enhance or even perfect. And I am still me.

My Monte Cristo hat with the ornaments stays on a closet shelf. I don't have to wear my hat to think.

I wear a shirt lined with flannel in true red whose color name did not come from an opera or even a play.

I dress for the day in warm, cotton corduroy slacks.

My colorful handkerchief with a hand rolled edge represents my favorite painting, Auguste Renoir's masterpiece, *Luncheon of the Boating Party*. In a combination of colors, he portrays fourteen vibrant, diverse and elegant Parisians enjoying a Sunday outing along the Seine River. Among those are an art collector, an Italian journalist, a war hero, a wealthy painter, a fine actress and Renoir's wife. This handkerchief is more than a fashion accessory, but a celebration of beauty.

I wear athletic shoes that are popular beyond sports knowing that any shoe that fits me may pinch another and no one knows where. I can't put the left foot on the right foot. The basic navy color with white accents with the soles pulled into the uppers and the tongue blended with the collar makes the shoes more like wearable, moving sculptures and most importantly provide bounce to my walk.

My watch is tucked beneath my shirt. I look at my watch intermittently. The interim times that make up a significant part of my life is the reality. I find a balance between my productive life and my emotional life. I ignore my watch readings of 1:05, 2:11, 3:16, 4:22, 5:27, 6:33, 7:38, 8:44, 9:49, 10:55 and 12:00—all the times rounded to the minute, the hour to overlap. These times are worth noting because time is the ultimate luxury as I grow old.

No professional movers want to move our furnishings to the cabin because of the weight limit on the Rio Grande bridge at Elk Creek Ranch. With a stroke of luck we locate Jim Stromberg, a furniture maker, who will take our furnishings to the cabin. Two weeks before Christmas, with all our possessions for the cabin singled out, we load them into his stripped down thirty-six foot mobile home. It is full except for the trundle beds he will pick up in Lewisville, Texas, on the way to the cabin. He drives off with all our possessions and we don't hear from him again until two days after Christmas.

Jim hauls his mobile home with his father following in another truck in case he breaks down. When the movers arrive at our cabin, the ranch's caretaker says there is too much snow and can't help him get up the steep incline of our driveway. But Jim says that he will get up the hill because with him are his pregnant wife, five children, father, sleeping bags, and a microwave. He backs his mobile home up the driveway in three feet of snow. His family has Christmas in our living room.

When I finally call the cabin two days after Christmas, Jim answers the telephone, "Reily Residence." He says they have placed all our furniture using my diagram, Christmas morning is celebrated, and has it all cleaned up except the gift wrapping paper on the floor. They are officially our first guests.

Later Clauda and Jaím Baker give us an ordinary size guest book which is a sentimental remembrance custom of happy times and gatherings of family and friends. I place the guest book on the table by the front door where our guests, even in their departure, can sign with a sharp pen their names with a date and a quick note which is not always in rhyme. I enter Jim's name, date and his comments in the book as our first guest.

We open the cabin door just after dark on Wednesday, December 30, 1987. Lots of planning on my part and seven or eight trips to our site over one and one-half years makes this possible.

As we move in, the winter wind has sneaked into the corners of our lives and we try to make the best of it as it blows down the valley bringing refreshing times. It is only minus twenty degrees below zero and the refrigerator is not connected. I leave my ice chest outside. With no draperies on our bedroom window we see a clear, nearly full moon and wait for the morning light breaking through from the east.

The next day, New Year's Eve, with all the boxes to unpack we manage breakfast with no plates. We begin placing our furnishings. We hang a mirror on the back wall of the living room so that anyone facing that wall will have a view of the mountain at their back, a mirror to nature. Could it be the mirror is our best friend? It provides a dialogue between the exterior and interior. It expands the area to offer the illusion of wide open space even though the living room is small. Even with a candle lit in front of the mirror light is spread. The sofa and chairs by the fireplace are covered in different pattern green fabric that relate to the landscape's earth colors of green and brown. Native American rugs cover the vinyl floor.

With no formal rules for hanging art because the eye is the beholder, we keep the architecture foremost in our minds. We hang art at the universal eye-level height. Two Joseph Imhof paintings are hung on each side of the fireplace with no direct light on them.

Building the cabin is literally a trail of very few disappointments in hundreds of details.

I leave the cabin, hopefully, with no one noticing, because I've done something worthwhile which is true happiness.

Earlier I began another writing trail that lasted almost twenty years. Initially, the only qualification I owned for writing Joseph A. Imhof's biography was that I knew him. But as the trail progressed I acquired the two requirements for a biographer: research and writing. The early trails of research led to my first New Mexico Art History Conference in Taos, New Mexico where I met art historians.

In the days before every corner of the world was accessible from my desk with Google, my research about Imhof and his wife, Sallie, continued in other institutions. In Fort Worth at the Amon G. Carter Museum I opened the Imhof file to discover the first item was a July, 1952 *Denver Post* newspaper article and photograph featuring Joe and me at the grand opening of my Aunt Helen and Uncle Winfield's Grand Imperial Hotel in Silverton, Colorado. This startling discovery opened a trail I never considered: that not only was I seeking Imhof but Imhof was seeking me. The writing trail developed into another way to see and express, similar to Joe's artist brush. The writing trail with its starts, stops and detours led me to change intellectual passion to physical energy and narrative mastery.

I only continued Sallie's work. In one of her letters directing Joe's archives, Sallie described him: "Joe was a gentle, dignified man who loathed the publicity and the limelight that other artists seemed to seek; he avoided publicity at all times, but I do understand that posterity through his collection should know something about the real Imhof."

My twenty-two years of friendship with Joseph Imhof and Sallie, plus fifty-four years of contact with the Imhof name, came together as Joe's biography after I devoted fifteen years of research and three and one-half years of writing with Lucille Enix: *Joseph Imhof, Artist of the Pueblos.*

When I researched the book I never wondered why I was writing the book. Now that the book is completed I never ask myself why I wrote it. However, for just a touch of humor I am amused if asked the simple question, "Did you write the book or type it?"

I am considered an authority on Imhof, but I know an authority is someone fifty miles from home with Power Point.

I felt like I was at the top of my game and now the challenge was to stay at the top. With the aspect of being a published writer, there was no invasion of privacy that accompanies fame which can be a reason to retreat. I was recognized but not enough for a life size cardboard cut-out made of me for posing with tourists. I was famous in a small way which meant that the only difference was people who are famous, more people knew their name. I realized I didn't have to be perfect to experience the thrill of achievement.

Friday, January 1, 1988, South Fork—Don and I are starting a new year in a new home. It's a home we've talked of and planned for years. We wave good-bye to 1987. We worked all day putting things in order and we still have empty shelves everywhere. Judy and Walter Skinner came down at 6:00 pm for cocktails, our first guests. Then we went to their house for blackeyed peas, cornbread and ham. Black-eyed peas are supposed to bring good luck for the New Year. I changed my annual "goals" to "directions" because goals can limit.

Tuesday, September 13, 1988, Lufkin, Texas—It is very rewarding to have spent my spare time in such a way, but scary. Writing is a means of expression but to publish is to publicly express. Now that I'm here, I'm not sure I want to publish. It will reveal that I have sensitiveness, understanding the building blocks of life, that I don't have all the solutions and I have much to learn. Perhaps, as I progress into publishing, my way will be clearer as to whether to publish or not.

Friday, December 31, 1988, Dallas, Texas—The last day of a very full year and we rang in the New Year on the dance floor, one of my favorite places. As traumas, some were expected and some unexpected, entered our family we are reminded again of how fragile life is. I close the year with a grateful heart.

Mother had been managing Archie in her home as a one-woman nursing home. With a broken hip, he lost the ability to walk.

He never lost his eyesight, but if he had, his mind could bring forth images. Just before 1988 ended, the sandwich generation lessened when my stepfather, Archie, died. When Mother and I went to the hospital he recognized us, but could barely respond. The doctor told us, as we knew, that there was no treatment that could reverse the process. He was dying and the doctor told us that he would be surprised if he made the day. I left Mother for an hour to be alone with her husband of thirty-one years, longer than how long she had been married to my father. He then went into a coma and he must have sensed that he could let go. He went peacefully. Archie always wanted a quick death and joked about it, but he hung on for a long time. He just thought he was ready to go, but he wasn't.

His funeral services were to be grave side in Vega, Texas. The funeral director gathered all the family in one room and with a blood red face said complications had occurred. The grave had been dug, the vault on site, but not in place, no tent or chairs set up because the man in charge had quit mid-job. The funeral director had the Baptist church opened, hired an organist who had to take curlers out of her hair, moved the casket, set up the flowers and would have someone at the grave site to direct people to the church. We looked at each other in disbelief and Mother made the classic remark, "I wish it had been the Methodist church." We buried a good, honest, honorable man who would have enjoyed all the Murphy's Law commotion.

Mother said, "We have had a lot of good and will have to take the sad, too."

On Saint Patrick's Day in 1988, Don and I enter into a birthing room to see Donna as she is beginning labor for our fifth grandchild. My daughter is doing fine and so am I, this time. Just as she is born, the nurse takes Donna's fingerprints. Minutes after the baby is born the nurse makes the baby's footprints and places them on the same page of paper for the hospital records. The baby has fair skin and hazel/brown eyes. My second granddaughter always celebrates on Saint Patrick's Day with emerald green. She carries her fraternal grandfather's mother name and her father's mother's maiden name—Julia Archer Davis. Julia will mature on the radiant side of beautiful.

To my Monte Cristo hat I add a 2 1/2 x 2 inch turquoise and silver pin featuring three leaf-like designs and two branch-like designs with stones on each branch.

With her godparents present to give sincere care, Julia is christened in the same dress that Mark, Donna and Carolyn wore. Julia's initials are embroidered in the hem. Now the dress continues a family history. Julia is restless before the ceremony at the Church of the Good Shepherd, but settles down when the event begins. She is honored with a luncheon in her home.

This celebrated fifth grandchild is indeed another gift, a present. I am a grandmother now with much tolerance. She teaches us the habits of the heart that keep all our grandchildren fresh in our hearts. In time Julia and Carolyn entertain each other as if they are the same age.

As with all our grandchildren, our role is to comfort and provide a safe harbor, but not undercut the parents. We can spoil only with love, take pride in their good qualities, and not be responsible for every act and trait. Julia can handle all the love we can give her. She puts no obstacles in our way to let us love her. I know that she will have the opportunities everyone assumes she will have. She carries herself with elegance—a trait that can't be hurried. We know she will uphold courteous manners although the world's times are showing lack of refinement. No summer will be complete without a mosaic of fun times with Julia.

Julia's vision is the ability to see. She will be able to see what has been, what is, and what will be and more importantly to see why things are as they are. We share a love of design which guarantees a bond and specialness.

Julia is saying lots of words and quite curious. Donna bought her a bowl of goldfish. Donna said that she often found Julia with her lips resting on the edge of the bowl and her shirt wet. Donna suspects that Julia is probably sipping the gold fish water.

When Julia was two and one-half years old the unexpected happened. She breaks her right thigh bone and is in a body cast from her toes to shoulders. I am at the cabin when Donna and Don fly her to the cabin because the heat in her hometown of Corpus Christi is intolerable. Tears come to my eyes when Julia crawls to her trundle bed, pulls herself up as far as she can and says, "Help me Mother."

I enjoy reading to Carolyn and Julia when they are in bed for the night. Holding a book is like a baby's contact with his favorite blanket. Julia always wants me to read *Where's Waldo*. I hold the large hardback version because it is more solid, weightier and more permanent. There are hundreds of figures on the page and the object is to find Waldo on each page. Carolyn, being older, can find Waldo easily. But Julia compensates as I begin turning the page, sits up, doesn't say a word, and begins looking for Waldo before I turn the page.

Julia notes Donna's portrait when she was a little girl. Julia says "That was Mother when she was little, but now it's me."

Julia and I have a dialogue about television. When I tell her that when I was little I didn't have television but listened to the radio, she asks, "When you listened to the radio, what did you look at?"

Jane and Mark are expecting their fourth child. They do not tell whether it is a boy or girl, but when they paint a room pink, we suspect the gender.

Eighteen days after Julia's birth, Mark in his scrubs, comes out of the delivery room in Houston, beaming over the birth of his daughter and our third granddaughter—Anna Catherine Reily. She is named Anna after my mother who is named after her mother's sister, and Catherine, a name her parents like. Anna is on the patrician side of beautiful.

With my mother's namesake I have all the happiness without all the stress of being the mother. Anna is carrying a family name, her genes, and her spirit into new times. It's easy to stand back and let the parents have the chance. She is part of a family that can weather disagreements and stressful times because the grandparent and parent relationship is strong but not overlapping.

My Monte Cristo hat now displays a round 1 1/2 x 1 inch turquoise and silver pin shaped like a turtle with nine stones. This is the last of my grandchildren and the last pin to decorate and anchor down my hat.

As Anna changes her view of the world from the floor where she rolls over and plays, she and I will share a love of written words and seeing through the camera's eye. One leads to the other in a natural progression.

When my sixth grandchild is born, I am middle-age and I adapt to the next lessons in life by being an example rather than a lecturer. I still organize, not agonize and I am admitted to the room.

Read and Thomas go with Don and me to see their new sister. They look at Anna in the incubator and from the look on their faces, they are in awe and don't know what it is all about. Jane and Mark have their girl. When Mark, Anna and Jane come to their home from the hospital, there is a huge sign in their yard, "Congratulations, It's a Girl, Anna Catherine," The boys take their mother some flowers in a vase they have painted.

When we arrive home from the hospital and Anna's birth, the weather is chilly, so I ask Mark to get me some long pants for Read, Thomas and John who I am keeping while Jane and Mark adjust to having Anna at home for the first time. Mark in gathering their long pants can't remember whose clothes belong to whom. He then turns to me and says with a laugh, "I've got so many children I don't even know which is their room."

Anna will glean and process the world's information long before she can tell us what she knows. But I know not only do girls need us, but that we need them. She moves with elegance which is a kind of intelligence. She dares to soar.

As a baby Anna can handle all the love we can give her. As with all our grandchildren, they put no obstacles in our way to let us love her.

Anna is christened into the visible church at the First United Methodist Church in Lufkin wearing a long white dress that one of Jane's friends bought in Europe. I don't look directly at Anna because lately she tenses. Mark holds John Mark, Jane holds Anna. Anna doesn't cry when the minister holds her up high for all to see. At the altar Thomas strolls away and Read kneels on the kneeling bench. When Thomas comes back to his father, Mark very tenderly puts his hand on his shoulder. John, when they left the altar, utters, "Da-Da, Dot, Dot."

Anna calls me Papa because she can't say Grandmother. She finally masters Grandmother in a plain, mannerly way. When she begins to talk, she says "thank you" to every remark.

Anna is crawling everywhere and when her brothers open the bottom drawers of their chests of drawers, Anna makes a dash for them to pull out all their pajamas.

Anna is walking everywhere and Julia is still crawling. When we put them together we think Julia will walk, but instead Anna gets on the floor and crawls with Julia.

Anna teaches us the wonder of a daily walk with her and the other five grandchildren, that even if all are crying, it is okay.

Anna knows that she can sit in the living room to socialize with us. She soon questions our manners—do you put your napkin on the table or in your chair when you leave the dining table?

The dinner table gives meaning to the word "family."

Anna is at the breakfast room table with all the family. We are served from the kitchen buffet. Don sits at the table and says, "Let's say the blessing before we eat." With that Anna puts down her fork and takes the food out of her mouth and places the food on her plate.

When she is old enough we take her to the country club for dinner with John Mark. Don asks Anna, "Are you left-handed?" Anna replies, "No, I am two." She then adds, "Look John Mark. There are two forks."

She wants to play with us when she is young, which gives us a few special years. She makes us chuckle about our foibles. After that we run after her and then she comes back to us. In her youth she will be close to her siblings, grow apart later, and to become closer as they all age.

As a grandparent I am a human resource holding families together as a surrogate mom. I am a spiritual guide. With a serene example, I am just there and not cropped out of the portrait changing the dynamics of an American family. My grand babies go where I carry them.

We don't know it, but this will be our sixth and last grandchild which makes me an empathetic grandmother. It is still considered a gift, a present. If neglect enters, these grandchildren drop out of our awareness. It is a habit of the heart that keeps them fresh in our lives.

We may break the rules which distresses our children, but they must remember that we don't make the rules, the parents make the rules. We give them the right to think without speaking, not to speak without thinking.

Our grandchildren easily help us appreciate the wonder of our daily walk. I share experiences with them and when they touch my skin they recognize that my skin is old and yet honorable. And that I look much prettier under a pink light bulb. They don't know that when their grandfather and I do something stupid like losing our car keys, that we tell each other, "Don't tell the children."

When I celebrate the birthday for one, I bake six small cakes complete with candles. After singing *Happy Birthday* to the honored one, Jane and I let them eat into the cake with a fork rather than cut them a slice. After the mess, Jane and I have cake all over us. Jane says, "You just become one of them."

I have all my grandchildren for dinner and we have hamburgers by candlelight. They ask, "What are the candles for?" I tell them they are for atmosphere and that we are all going to have a dinner all seated together. I ask them, "Does everyone have their napkin in their lap?" John Mark jumps out of his chair to crawl under the table. When he comes up he exclaims, "Everyone has their napkin in their lap."

John Mark learns how to swing. Jane says that night she sits on the side of the bed and John says, "I hope I don't forget how to swing."

When Mark tells the family that he may be promoted in his banking position, we ask if he will get a salary raise. Mark doubts that he will. Thomas asks, "Dad, if you don't get a raise, can you ask for a nap?"

Read wants me to set an alarm for him because he says he has never gotten up with an alarm. But when Don's alarm goes off at 5:30 am Read must have heard it and comes to the bed and asks, "Is it time to get up?"

At Astro World Read keeps eyeing the Twist ride. Mark takes him on it. They get off "bug-eyed." Read says, "I don't think I will ride anything else I have to hold on to."

Everyday events in the life of six grandchildren: Read leans down to take Anna by the hand to help her. Read notices all my genealogy papers and asks, "Do you have any that go back to the pirates?" Thomas tells very long stories and is concerned over everyone getting their turn. John Mark gives good hugs and asks "Why?" to everything, then asks, "What is half-way? Can you count to a million? How long is ten minutes? And the ultimate at night when I sleep with him, wakes up and cries, "Where's Grandmother?" Anna smiles and sucks her thumb. When we celebrate Anna's birthday with all the family and my mother, Thomas hands Anna a card from my mother who they call Mimi, and tells Anna, "This one is from Mimi and my card from Mimi has money in it." Carolyn and Julia call "shot gun." All six grandchildren visit the Lufkin zoo with me.

When we keep all six grandchildren at one time we have the time and resources, yet we know we are outnumbered. We are hoping for controlled chaos without building a corral. Yet, we are overwhelmed with enjoyment. We are happy to do it now because when they grow older we may not have the opportunity. Our hearts ache to see them and anticipation awaits us for the next time to see them.

Now that the grandchildren are older, there are less crying moments, but play hard and they have a good time. I feel like the house has been stirred, the clocks have all been tampered with, pens are missing from their holders by the telephone, and toys are scattered. Everything gets rearranged, but we do survive it to appreciate the "life" our grandchildren bring to us.

All my grandchildren are born and christened and will develop character which is no more than trustworthiness, respect, responsibility, fairness, caring and citizenship. They are a treasure of affection. I cannot ask for more. I renew my commitment to their needs. I know their moral strength passes from one generation to the next.

Sunday, January 1, 1989, Dallas, Texas—My diary for 1989 begins as a blank page in a blank book. I've never tried to recycle last year's diary by using the same last year's pages for this year. I would be confronted with entries of the past. Although I find it beneficial to reflect, I only need to deal with "today" and possibly "tomorrow." My diary reading will be a way of entertaining me in my later years. Just the reading of my times and growth will be my reward. My diary entries may be the single remnant of my heritage. I've observed and recorded my time in its surroundings even if I didn't make history. As a spin-off my diary is a means of self-definition. It's an easy way to grapple with who I am while I deal with the ordinariness of errands and chores.

Sunday, December 31, 1989, Lufkin, Texas—There is a feeling that hope is in the air for the world. What better way to end a year and decade. America is no longer "center stage," the economy is global, our American baby boomers are middle age now and are involved with building the family. Family is still as important as ever in the larger family environment.

Maybe our days of "what about me" are maturing into "what about us." Values got out of whack but the values of self-made individualism and the desire for caring and community are trying to get back in sync. It seems like a good way to begin a new year.

Monday, January 1, 1990, Lufkin, Texas—A new year begins and a new decade begins. No successful trend setter so far has named this decade, the 1990s, before it begins.

Monday, September 17, 1990, Lufkin, Texas—This week promises to be slower paced than last week which is good. Don and I can still manage a fast-paced week but we have to give it more thought. I went to Garland Picou Treatment Center for my back. Halfway through my treatment, Don called, saying to call him but that it wasn't an emergency. I called and he told me Doris Bowman was trying to reach me because two advance copies of *I Am At An Age* had arrived. I called Doris to tell her I'd be over in forty-five minutes and asked, "How do they look?" She said, "The outside looks good, but I haven't taken off the plastic wrap. I thought you'd want to do that!"

I finished my treatment and went over to Best of East Texas publishers. The book looked great and I opened one copy and told Doris to open the other. I felt like this wasn't really happening but it was. I didn't know how I was going to feel, but I felt awed. The dust jacket colors printed true and made a clear statement. The combination of colors appeal to any eye, the black print on the dust jacket inside the flaps printed crisp over the pastels, the white spine had no overlap onto the back cover, my name in the blue black was distinguishable and my photo printed darker and grainier, but I was not disappointed in anything. The inside paper color was soft and easy on the eye, the margins wide enough, the print large and wide and only a slight hint of the print on back of the pages on the blank spots of the pages. I had tried to prepare myself for any unexpected surprises but there were none that I could find. Doris and I examined the book. I thanked her repeatedly and she told me that I was easy to work with. She said she thought Don would come with me but I told her "You know how that goes!" Mary Byrd, Nita Marsellos and Earlon Williams came in to buy a book but the remaining 998 books won't be in until the last of the week. I went home and Don greeted me with enthusiasm. We talked about the book. Don told me it was beautiful in a voice that rang of sincerity. He read the Prologue and said, "This is me—give away more." I told him my thoughts applied to men and women but few men would probably read it.

Don went back to work. I ate my lunch and sat down in the Lazy-Boy chair to look through my first book. I was not sure I wanted to read it again, but I opened the book, read the Prologue and tears started rolling down my cheeks. It read of emotional content, not grammatical errors. I knew I couldn't read any more without crying and I wanted the day to be "of this day" not "of reflection." It's hard to believe, in one way, that this is my book, but when I read it I knew it was because I lived through the events and the writing of the events. That makes it mine. I called to thank Lucille Enix and Jeanelle McCall. I called Donna but she wasn't home, so I left a message and she called at night. I took my book to Mother and she told me how proud of me she was. Don and I celebrated at the cafeteria and rented the video "Blaze" because nothing was better on at the theaters. Today was a reserved day, BUT WHAT A DAY!"

I had made the decision to let go of the book and publish. But the market for unknown writers was limited because few greet unpublished writers with acceptance. The alternate of rejection slips was to co-publish with my decisions of the aesthetics of font, spacing, paper and deadlines. Co-publishing was only a series of actions as creator, designer, printer, marketer, sales person and business manager. I had control of the book, but with the privilege of making mistakes.

Tuesday, September 25, 1990, Lufkin, Texas—Don got me up early because I wanted to be dressed early. I was hoping my books would be delivered early. At 10:00 am Wendy Williams called that they had arrived. I called Don, Jane and Mark and then went to the office of Best of East Texas Publishers on South First Street. My heart jumped as I saw the truck being unloaded—so many boxes, I thought—what have I done! Mark walked over from North Carolina National Bank (NCNB). Doris Bowman was busy with a client, so Mark and I opened the first box. The box had Styrofoam peanuts on top of the books because it was a partially filled box. Mark brushed off the peanuts and pulled out the book and smiled. I think he'd been dubious about my writing a book, so I was pleased he pulled out the first one. Mark smiled and said how pretty it was. The office was busy. Doris said I'd been asked to be on a radio talk show and I thought she was teasing me. Mark went back to the bank. Jane, John Mark and Anna came by. John Mark looked in the box full of peanuts and asked Jane,

"Would it be stealing if I got some peanuts?" Jane said, "No." John Mark filled Jane's purse with peanuts. Don came and took photographs. I autographed the seventy-five books we'd already sold. The day was a great sense of accomplishment and pride. I enjoyed sharing it with my family. I went home to lunch and back to autograph books. I took Mother her copy and she expressed her pride. I presented Don his copy and he began reading it in the evening. We had dinner at the cafeteria. I went to bed exhausted from joy.

I enjoyed the comments on *I Am At An Age*:

Mother: How did you think all this up? I knew you were smart, but not that smart.

Frances Young: Nancy sure is smart.

Jane Cornelius: I read until 1:00 am, told Raymond he needed to read this chapter and want to read it again.

Dr. Willis told Mother: I didn't know you had an author in the family.

Don: I was at Brookshire Brothers grocery store on Monday getting my mother's weekly *National Inquirer, Star, Globe* and *TV Guide* when a man told me, "Here your wife has written a book and you're buying *National Inquirer*." Don said that it was for his mother and the man said "Sure!"

Jim Williams: The book is great, a real challenge to read, so few books are a challenge to read.

Garland Picou: I'm reading your book and enjoying it. Let me put it this way, I've always liked you, but I envy you that you can reveal another side of yourself.

Joanne Hallmark: I was keeping him [Kenzy] up nights reading my book.

Jenny Fleming: She didn't know there was anyone that intelligent in Lufkin.

The Appletree grocery store checker: Hi to Lufkin's newest celebrity.

Bill Royle: Hi, authoress.

Carolyn Werner: It's a marvelous experience.

Mayor Pitser Garrison: He is really enjoying it because it's a person book.

Sonny Clements: I admire you for your courage.

My brother Morten Hopkins: We have the same values that come from our parents.

Doris Bowman: Anyone who doesn't enjoy it is not very smart; one person said it was racy.

Waldenbooks asked if I was interested in an autograph session.

Judge Jaím Baker: I'm reading it slowly as my legal mind doesn't read metaphors easily.

Raymond Cornelius: Congratulations on your book.

Marietta Moreau: I'm saving it for after Christmas.

Margot Hundley: I enjoyed your book.

James Windham: It's over my head.

Buddy Rush: I want an autographed copy for my son.

Mrs. Jesse Johnston: The cover is lovely, such soft colors.

Louise Maxwell: You are so open, honest—very few people can take off their masks.

Annabelle Henson: Your book is interesting, unique.

Maggie Green DeNike: Nancy is smarter than me, deeper than me and she can spell.

I was pleased that men were reading my book in addition to women. The last few weeks, I enjoyed these comments. I took all this with a "grain of salt," but it was nice to hear, anyway. Fame was not the end of my story, but today was the best time. Besides, it didn't hurt to examine my life.

I was fifty-six years old in 1990 when I published my first book, *I Am At An Age*. My September 25, 1990 daily journal entry expressed myself with openness, spontaneity and in a different language than when I write for a purpose. I wanted to stay my age, act my age and live my age. I knew *I Am At An Age* was ready for you, the general audience, who in my imagination is safe in your development of reading readiness, word mastery, vocabulary growth and reading maturity. I had not written in the margins of my life but in the first person pronoun, "I." I was eager to declare myself. My small bit of fame meant doing the work to find out who I was, so I don't define myself by what others say and write about me.

That same September my joy accompanied the responsibility to place my book in the proper location in my book shelves. Interior decorators place books as to color, height and length. But a writer places the books carefully like placing guests at a dining table. My library books are organized for pleasure and convenience according to autobiographies, memoirs, inspirational, fiction, nonfiction, instructional and even trash. My bookshelves are located in the faraway living room in shelves with air circulating around them, in the closer family room where the shelves began as empty, but the books came, and, lastly, on the closer bedside table for books that knew they were in their proper place.

As the master of my personal library, how did I know where to place, *I Am At An Age*? For the book's integrity did I classify the writing as an autobiography, memoir or inspirational?

Perhaps, my writing was an autobiography, but not in the true sense because my autobiography should be written close to the end of my life to be as near the end of the story as possible. Yes, an autobiography if it explains how I became Nancy Carolyn Hopkins Reily. I didn't feel like I was Caucasian, woman, wife, mother, daughter, sister, sister-in-law, mother-in-law, grandmother, Protestant, citizen and educated. I felt like I was just myself as I wrote of myself. No, I didn't think of the book as an autobiography because I am an ordinary individual.

Is my book a memoir? Yes, as a memoir should be fragments of sensibilities of a life geared to a central theme because how the life story ends is an unknown. Yes, in that my tone of writing covering forthright actions tells of my life's ages by capturing universal experiences understood by all.

Is the book inspirational? Yes, in that inspiration comes from responsible communicating. An ordinary individual can, if he chooses, release that illusive, tiny part of his inward, energized self to become extraordinary for the moment.

To distance myself from the categorizing process I placed my book that crossed genre boundaries not on a shelf but between two bookends in the living room. The single book showed such loneliness that the other books alive in my imagination demanded completion.

With time I wrote seven more books. I even compiled all my recipes in a book when my grandchildren kept asking me how to cook certain foods. I accumulated books and more books for research and pleasure. My two book shelves were as full as I could manage. I used the top of the book shelves and double stacked some. When I decided to thin out my book shelves, I couldn't decide which books to get rid of—the fluffy, chick novels that I never read, the ones I reread frequently, the ones that touched my soul, the self-help books, the writing guides, the various dictionaries and thesauruses, the books that brought laughter, and those written by people I admired. In the end, I just added another book shelf.

When completed the several books I wrote, although varied in subject matter, would show the real growth process of my life.

I stated in a clear voice in the Prologue of *I Am At An Age*:

> To my son and daughter, while I am always your mother I would like for you to read me as a person. So be loving with your response, for this is how I learned.

I thought at age fifty-six I had learned all I needed to learn. Six months after publishing *I Am At An Age*, I realized I had more to learn. I continue to ask my children who are now in their fifties, and now my grandchildren who are in their twenties, to read me as a person. Be loving with your response because I am still learning.

Afterword

Tuesday, August 7, 2012, South Fork, Colorado – As Tuesday's child "full of grace," today is my seventy-eighth birthday. In my cabin home of twenty-four years, when I pull the Roman shades I am greeted by a clear view of the green trees against a cerulean blue sky. I think it is a hearty omen for a happy birthday although I am over one thousand miles from my home of forty-five years.

I am dressed appropriately in my shirt, slacks, handkerchief, shoes and watch. My Monte Cristo hat with six turquoise and silver pins is on the closet shelf ready to wear any time.

As I close this sequel to *I Am At An Age*, I appreciate how Jim Smith of Sunstone Press guided me when my writing took me places I didn't intend. Vicki Ahl and Carl Condit added their support.

This is the final entry for *Half-Past Winter, Second Beginnings: My Story, So Far*. I thought I could add more years to the story, but don't know how after publication. And then who would edit it and add the remaining years.

I memorized several of my mother's sayings so I could always carry them with me. My mother told me in her last years, "Nancy, if you live long enough you just about experience everything." As I age further, I recall my mother's advice, "Getting old is just giving up things such as spicy food, late night hours, but not giving up learning." The following years, hopefully, will only be a reminder of all I have learned such as compassion, love, caring, tough love, a grateful heart and many more emotions.

I cared enough about life to record it. Maybe someone who cares about life will enjoy reading it and be a caretaker of my efforts whether in the actual red journals, file cabinets of genealogy, printed copies of my journal excerpts housed in my files, or the memorabilia.

So, this morning during my best thinking time between wake-up time of 5:00 am and get-up time of 6:30 am, I decided to end my story today on my birthday at exactly my birth time of 5:13 pm.

Although my description of my homes has been in detail, I am reminded that my final home will be as if the main pole of a tent is removed and the canvas slowly billows to the ground, and I will be free of earthly existence.

My spirit will live on from now until the end of time as my story passes through the generations from one child to the next.

—Nancy Carolyn Hopkins Reily

Tuesday, August 7, 2012, 5:13 pm

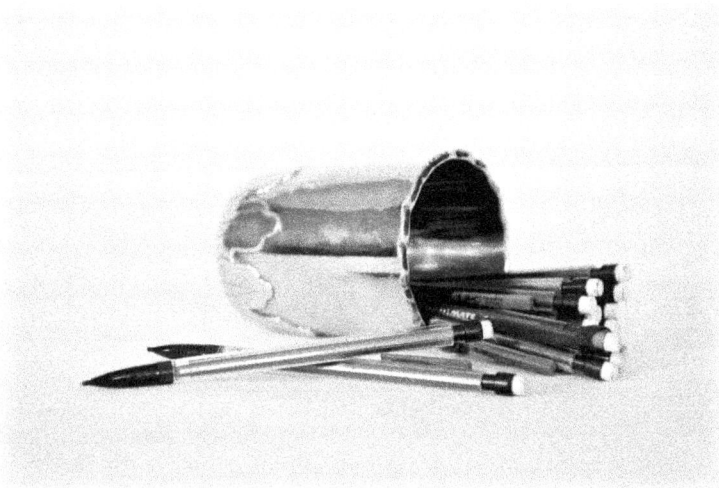

www.ingramcontent.com/pod-product-compliance
Lightning Source LLC
Chambersburg PA
CBHW021341090426
42742CB00008B/695